# Barry Goldwater:

## FREEDOM IS HIS FLIGHT PLAN

# Barry Goldwater:

## FREEDOM IS HIS FLIGHT PLAN

By Stephen Shadegg

Foreword by Clarence Budington Kelland

---

FLEET PUBLISHING CORPORATION

230 PARK AVENUE, NEW YORK 17, NEW YORK

# FOREWORD

It is not necessary to write a book to introduce Senator Barry Goldwater to the people of America, because there is no remote village North, South, East, or West in which his name is not a household word.

But it is well that citizens, who know him only as a Senator and a leader of conservative thought in the United States, should be made aware of the ancestral background which produced him and of the personal achievements and philosophies which have made of him one of the prime possibilities for election to the highest office in the gift of our people.

If one were to seek out and state the attributes which make him the personage he is, it would be necessary to place in the forefront integrity and courage. It would be necessary to number among his great abilities the power to analyze national events and to reach sound conclusions from facts, domestic and foreign, as they present themselves.

It is not enough that a political leader should be endowed with these qualities if he is to rise high in public estimation and affection. He must also number among his possessions personal charm and the ability to draw to himself the affection even of persons who have not enjoyed the privilege of his personal acquaintance.

It is to be doubted if, in all our history, there has existed a more diligent campaigner for the party which he honors by membership; nor a more sincere preaching of those high ideals which he believes will preserve the honor and stability and safety of our form of government which he reveres.

Barry Goldwater, though an Episcopalian himself, had a Jewish father. It is a splendid tribute to the decency of the American People that they have not regarded this as a disability, but indeed as an asset of value. It is a noble thing that the vigilantly Protestant South has taken him to its heart and that every sect of the North, even though sometimes in disagreement with him, bestows upon him the accolade of esteem. A scant dozen years ago it would have been impossible for a Goldwater even to be considered for the Presidency. The character and personality and fine intelligence of Barry Goldwater have made it not only possible but probable that, if he so desires, he will one day sit in the White House.

It has been my privilege to know intimately many of the great leaders and heroes of our country. There was, first and foremost, Herbert Hoover, then Robert Taft, Woodrow Wilson, these the outstanding political figures of the past two generations. Though younger and yet untried in their exalted positions, I consider the Arizona Senator fit to sit at table with them and to let his voice be raised in their company.

The word *Integrity* is not lightly to be bandied about; nor promiscuously be applied to this person or that person, because even the most exalted do not always bring to the furtherance of their ambitions clean hands. The word can be applied to Senator Goldwater because the conduct of his life has earned it. And even his bitterest opponent has never averred that his hands are not clean.

I hope this honest, sincere and scholarly biography by Stephen Shadegg will be as widely read as it richly deserves to be, and that the study of the events of his life and ancestry will add full measure to the admiration, esteem and affection in which our people hold Senator Barry Goldwater of Arizona.

—CLARENCE BUDINGTON KELLAND
*Oyster Bay, New York*

# CONTENTS

# ILLUSTRATIONS

## To Eugenia

Wife, sweetheart, helpful critic and constant inspiration without whose support this project could not have been completed.

# ACKNOWLEDGEMENTS

The writer is indebted to Senator and Mrs. Barry Goldwater, Mary Elizabeth Roush, Wilma Bennett, Harry Rosenzweig, Frank Kelley, Elva Wingfield, Bert Fireman, Ted Kazy, Marilyn Leopold, Robert Creighton, Carole Anne Theobald, Paul Sexson, Betty Rockwell, Newton Rosenzweig, Caroline Lynch, A. J. Bayless, Jack Williams, Ed McDowell, Fritz Marquardt, Edna Coerver and Dean Burch, whose assistance is reflected in whatever merit these pages possess.

# PREFACE

When cautious pilots prepare to leave this earth and soar through the skies to some far distant destination, they file with the Federal Aeronautics Administration what is called a flight plan.

The form is simple: point and time of departure, estimated arrival time, fuel on board, identification of the aircraft, pilot's home base and full name. This is a precautionary safety device. If the aircraft fails to arrive, a search is instituted and the flight plan gives a record of the pilot's intended course, altitude and fuel stops.

In this journey through life, millions of human beings live from day to day—an aimless, uncertain existence, never sure where they are going, frequently regretful of where they have been. Their time, without plan or purpose, is wasted. No man can be sure of where his life's journey will end or how long this trip will take, but each man is privileged in this Republic to select his own destination, to lay out his own course, to file his flight plan and reach for the stars.

Barry Goldwater, child of a Scotch-Irish woman of indomitable courage, grandson of an immigrant Polish peddler, is the inheritor of a great legacy of unshakeable faith in God and country. Barry, with clear and certain knowledge of all the forces in this world arrayed against individual freedom, has set forth on a course of service in support of those beliefs which created this Republic—*Freedom Is His Flight Plan.*

The reader of this book may conclude the writer is a strongly prejudiced admirer of United States Senator Barry Goldwater.

For more than ten years I have been in almost daily contact with this brilliant, determined young business man whose political personality has made so great an impression on this nation.

I have observed him in times of crises, moments of gaiety, in periods of sadness. I have seen him with his children and his wife, with his business associates, with his creditors, and with his political opponents. In my opinion, Barry Goldwater is dedicated to the preservation of the dignity of the individual and our constitutional Republic.

Because of what he is, what he has done, and what he is trying to do, he has earned my affectionate admiration; however, as I have been a journalist and reporter for many years, I am not blind to the human frailties of this gentleman.

The writing of Barry Goldwater's biography represents the fulfillment of an ambition. It is my hope this volume will not be regarded merely as a popular publication about an outstanding public figure. I have sought to present, in a way other Americans will understand, the warm, human qualities I've found in Barry; to permit you, the reader, to encounter the character of this individual, stripped of distortion and misinformation, so that you may share an understanding of his environment and the early nonpolitical years which have shaped and strengthened Barry Goldwater's determination: that freedom, expressed in a government of the people, by the people, and for the people, shall not perish from this earth.

—*Stephen Shadegg*
*Phoenix, Arizona*

# Barry Goldwater:

## FREEDOM IS HIS FLIGHT PLAN

CHAPTER **I**

## ONE TO NINETY

THE 1960 Convention of the Republican Party was, for the most part, a dull and listless affair. Apathetic delegates, assembled to rubber-stamp a *fait accompli*, exhibited very little genuine enthusiasm until the name of Barry Goldwater was presented to the convention.

The television cameramen and commentators, knowing full well this was no part of the script, did their best to minimize the delegates' reaction. Those in the hall and on the floor capable of objective judgement recognized they were witnessing something entirely out of character for the practical politicians of the GOP—a wild, exuberant, unlimited enthusiasm for a possible presidential candidate who had never been considered by the party rulers.

Ushers, blocking the aisles, forced the demonstrators outside and off the floor, and denied admittance to over three thousand young men and women who had come from all

19

over the nation to be present at the Stockyards for this
moment.

In 1960 only one percent of the nation's registered Republicans had ever heard the name Goldwater. There had
been no pre-convention campaign, no carefully planned program of publicity. His name had been placed in nomination
against his desire by the Governor of his native state. The
party hierarchy was solidly committed to Richard Nixon
whose nomination was signed, sealed and delivered months
before the delegates gathered in Chicago.

No one who was there can deny that at this moment the
tall, smiling, handsome figure of United States Senator Barry
Goldwater dominated the convention.

What is the quality in this man which permits him without
conscious effort to tower above the carefully engineered
images of so many of the accepted leaders of the Republican
Party?

A station wagon, bearing Arizona license plates, stops for
gasoline at a remote filling station in Cozad, Nebraska, and
the attendant eagerly beseeches, "Tell me about Barry Goldwater."

A Cajun fishing guide in Louisiana discovers that one
member of his tourist party is from Arizona. He says, "Mon-
sieur Barry Goldwater, un grand homme."

Newspaper men, clergymen, politicians, housewives, doctors, lawyers and merchants across the land have adopted
this lean, greying United States Senator from Arizona as
their symbol of hope for the future.

In all the past history of this republic it is difficult to find
a comparable figure. Arizona is politically unimportant, with
only four votes in the electoral college. Until 1950 there were
fewer than a million persons living within its borders, and

the Republican Party is still outnumbered there by two and one-half to one in registration.

A seat in the United States Senate is usually regarded as a political prize which must be earned by service in less exalted public positions. Barry Goldwater, who until he was forty-three years old had given no thought to a political career, grabbed this prize gold ring the first time he stepped on the political merry-go-round.

A Junior Senator from an unimportant Western state is ordinarily tolerated, but not listened to, in the world's greatest deliberative body. Goldwater's opinions and advice are earnestly sought by members with double his years of service.

Seven hundred thousand people have purchased copies of Goldwater's primer on his political philosophy, "The Conscience of a Conservative." On various campuses across the nation students carry copies to class. More than one hundred and fifty newspapers print his three-times-a-week essays on politics, morality, economics, and the mission of the Republican Party.

Members of the liberal press are dedicated to his destruction, and yet their grand vizirs concede that Goldwater followers constitute a force which may very well represent the strength of the Republican Party. Millions of plain Americans express gratitude for the life of this man. Probably the same number of citizens regard him with an antagonism they make no attempt to conceal, recognizing in the ideas he advocates the only viable threat to their plans for a central, socialist state.

In midsummer 1952, the odds against Barry Goldwater being elected to the United States Senate from Arizona were about five to one. In the forty year period beginning in 1912, when the state was admitted to the union, only one Republican had been elected to the Senate, and that single victory was a part of the Harding landslide of 1920.

The Goldwater name was distinguished and well-known throughout the state, but the family prominence was associated with its pioneer mercantile establishments. It is true that Barry's Uncle Morris, an old-line Jeffersonian Democrat, had been a member of the Constitutional Convention and successful in local Prescott politics. But this fact was actually a liability to his nephew, since a departure from the family Democrat tradition engendered active animosity in the minds of many Democrats and produced a similarly unfavorable reaction among many Republicans who believed that unless you were born to the party, your loyalty should be questioned.

On the plus side, the new Republican candidate for the Senate was affectionately known as "Barry" by thousands of his fellow Arizonans who had encountered him in business and civic affairs. He had served with distinction in World War II as a pre-Pearl Harbor volunteer. He was an acknowledged expert on matters pertaining to the division of Colorado River water, a matter of prime concern in this water-short state.

Goldwater's two terms on the Phoenix City Council were remembered with gratitude by his fellow residents of the capital city, but sectional jealousies turned this experience into a liability so far as the out-state counties were concerned.

As campaign manager for the successful Republican gubernatorial aspirant, Howard Pyle, in 1950, Barry had developed a sensitive antenna with which to measure the public mood. He was extremely conscious of the practical considerations predicting defeat.

Some men undertake the challenge of apparently insurmountable odds with a sort of Beau Geste fatalism, pretending to ignore the odds, and closing their minds to an acceptance of probable disaster. Barry cherished no illusions about the realities of the battle he faced. I had discussed with Barry the brutal statistics of the overwhelming Democratic Party registration. We were both aware of the percentages, and of the number which must defect to grant us victory.

"I'm not kidding myself about this," he told me in our first conversation when he was soliciting my services as campaign manager, "but we've reached a point where the people are entitled to make a meaningful choice between candidates. The New Deal and the Fair Deal have been taking us headlong down the road to state socialism. I may not be elected, but believing as I do about the future of freedom, I'll be damned if I'm going to surrender without putting up a battle."

Seven years later, long after the bone weariness of that 1952 campaign had been edged out of his memory by the happy recollection of victory, the same willingness to challenge apparently insurmountable odds produced what many observers believe to be the most dramatic reversal in the history of the United States Senate.

A valuable insight into Goldwater's character can be gained by studying him in action in the political arena.

On Wednesday, April 15, 1959, the United States Senate was opened with a prayer by the Rev. William C. Martin, Bishop of the Dallas-Fort Worth area of the Methodist Church.

With the Vice President presiding, the Majority Leader, Mr. Johnson of Texas, made his usual request for unanimous consent to dispense with the reading of the Journal for Monday, April 13.

The Junior Senator from Arizona was at his desk on the Republican side of the aisle. His face was tanned and healthy looking. Behind his horn-rimmed glasses there was a hint of weariness around the corners of his eyes. As he carefully read the annotated file in front of him, his lips tightened. More than two years of hearings; hundreds of thousands of words of testimony; the now sullen, now pleading faces of the witnesses before the McClellan Committee, were much more of a reality to him than the routine business of the Senate this morning.

As the members strolled casually to their places, pausing to visit or to exchange good-natured quips with their fellows, the Senator from Arizona found himself engulfed by a sense of despair, for what was scheduled to take place in these chambers would make all the earnest effort of the past two years an exercise in futility.

To Barry Goldwater, a man of direct action, the impotence of right and truth to be heard was like a physical weight resting on his own square shoulders.

In seven years he had come to know the body of men before him. The illusions he had brought to Washington had been shattered by the grubby realities of practical politics. Every man in that chamber was fully aware of the brutal abuses practiced by a handful of willful labor tyrants. No man among them would defend a Johnny Dio or a Jimmy Hoffa. Dave Beck, the once proud, arrogant boss of the Teamsters, had been revealed as a petty tyrant, a thief who had robbed the union treasury. Emil Mazey, the confident, glib, second-in-command of the UAW, had snarlingly accused all of the Roman Catholic clergy in three Wisconsin towns of a total lack of integrity during testimony before the McClellan Committee.*

Thousands of union members had written the Committee petitioning Congress to protect them against the tyranny of perpetual trusteeships, union bosses who looted union treasuries, arbitrary imposition of union dues, favoritism on job assignments, rigged strike elections. Working men begged for the right to criticize union affairs without risking death at the hands of hoodlums on the payrolls of union bosses.

Goldwater looked around the room, hoping to find on the face of a single Senator some tell-tale indication of understanding—of awareness that freedom on this day was hanging in the balance. He noted that John F. Kennedy, the Junior Senator from Massachusetts, was at his desk appearing confident. The Kennedys, John and his younger brother Bobby, who served as chief counsel for the hearings, had skillfully controlled the direction of inquiry. They had been able to stop any real searching into the activities of their friend Walter Reuther and his United Automobile Workers Union.

The shadow of Jack Kennedy's ambition to be President had blocked the efforts of the minority members of the Committee to examine carefully the brutal strike record of the UAW.**

In the chambers, dour-faced John McClellan, who had

---

* Speech of Hon. Carl T. Curtis of Nebraska, Congressional Record, Wed., March 26, 1958.

** The committee assigned only one investigator, in addition to the minority counsel, to examine the Kohler and Perfect Circle strikes. The full staff had been assigned to Hoffa and the Teamsters. The committee, in executive session, blocked an inquiry into the alleged corrupt practices of UAW official Richard Gosser.

endured the abuse and vilification heaped upon him by the labor racketeers and their lawyers with great forebearance, appeared to be unaware that on this day the Senate was prepared to make a mockery of all his sincere and determined efforts.

On the Republican side of the aisle, Senators Javits and Kuchel were engaged in earnest conversation. They would, Goldwater shrewdly guessed, support the Kennedy proposal.

John Foster Dulles was dying of cancer. His resignation was read to the Senate by the Majority Leader. There were words of praise from Dirksen of Illinois, Mansfield of Montana, Morton of Kentucky, Keating of New York, Wiley of Wisconsin, Kuchel of California, and Neuberger of Oregon—Neuberger who was soon to die of cancer himself.

The fact that some of these who spoke so glowingly of the dying Secretary had bitterly attacked and opposed him in these same chambers was lost or ignored in the sentimental eulogies.

Senator Hayden, powerful chairman of the Appropriations Committee, asked for forty million dollars to be added to the fund of the Department of Labor, and, without objection, that sum was allocated. No one seemed to know or care or even understand any longer that each million dollars so spent had to be extracted by the tyranny of the tax collector from the sweat and the toil of the helpless individual citizen caught in the vise between an ever-increasing cost of living and ever-increasing taxes.

With these preliminaries out of the way, the Vice President declared the morning business to be ended.

The Senate expressed no interest in the $112,000 that was to be spent by the Committee on Armed Services for repairs, alterations and improvements of the Naval Reserve Building in Boston.

The Administrator of the VA transmitted a draft of proposed legislation to modernize pension programs.

Alaska asked that the Federal government make payments in lieu of taxes for land and property occupied in that new state.

Hawaii desired a veterans' home because "veterans of the Korean conflict are fast approaching their twilight years."

The American Federation of Labor, through Senator Humphrey of Minnesota, expressed a desire for established federal standards in state unemployment compensation programs.*

Mr. Javits of New York asked to have included in the record a resolution adopted by the Veterans of Foreign Wars of Dutchess County favoring the reactivation of the Castle Point Veterans Hospital.

Some thirty pages of record were thus occupied before Senator Barry Goldwater of Arizona was recognized to ask unanimous consent to have the views prepared by the staff of the minority of the McClellan Committee, in connection with the Labor-Management Reporting and Disclosure Act of 1959, printed in the body of the Record.

No one objected. It almost seemed as if no one listened; no one cared, but the galleries were beginning to fill. The Senate pages moved in and out of the chamber.

---

* Mr. Humphrey of Minnesota asked unanimous consent that a resolution adopted on April 8, 1959 by the St. Paul AFL-CIO Trades and Labor Assembly in support of legislation H.R. 3547 and S. 791 to set certain federal standards in connection with the state unemployment compensation programs be inserted in the record saying: "I am proud to be a co-sponsor of this legislation which is sorely needed in order to provide adequate benefit payments to our country's unemployed workers." Page 5882, Congressional Record, Senate.

Senator Humphrey claimed the floor to remark that Dr. Fidel Castro, the leader of the new Cuban Revolution, would arrive in the United States surrounded by honorable men who were the advisers in his government.

The Senator from Minnesota warned against this nation's failure to understand the social revolution, and introduced for the Record a nine-point program, concluding with the statement: "Let us hope that we will be able to convey our deeply-felt best wishes to Fidel Castro and the Cuban people for the full realization of their aspirations for a democratic and progressive Cuba."

Finally, the Senate inched its way forward to the business of the moment—the consideration of Senate Bill 1555, described as "A bill to provide for the reporting and disclosure of certain financial transactions and administrative practices of labor organizations and employers to prevent abuses in the administration of trusteeships by labor organizations. To provide standards with respect to the election of officers of labor organizations, and for other purposes."

The title was happy and all-inclusive. It seemed to recognize the existence of evils and to call for adequate legislative correction. In the debates to come the measure would be referred to either by number or as the Kennedy-Ervin Bill.

This was it, the moment of drama suddenly on center stage dwarfing the routine which had preceded it. The Senate galleries were full. John Kennedy rose to make his opening statement.

"Mr. President, today we begin debate on Senate Bill 1555, the labor-management Reporting and Disclosures Act for 1959. Before we proceed with the discussion of the provisions of this bill and a debate on its merits, I would like to review very briefly for the Senate the background of this measure."

Senator Kennedy was speaking for the Record. The members present exhibited little interest and the Massachusetts Senator made no demand for their undivided attention.

"More than two years ago the Senate by resolution established a bipartisan select committee to look into improper activities in the labor-management field.

"The select committee, popularly known as the McClellan Committee, was established because of recurring reports of abuses of power on the part of both labor and management to the detriment of the welfare of the employees, employers and the public.

"For more than two years now under the able leadership of the distinguished Senator from Arkansas," there was a pause to emphasize the offering of a compliment, "this committee has looked into various situations which have been brought to its attention in an effort to spotlight problems requiring legislation."

Then followed a recital of statistics on the hearings until finally, modestly and without rancor, the Senator from Massachusetts commented that the measure was originally drafted by two members of the McClellan Committee in 1958—former Senator Ives of New York and himself. Then said Senator Kennedy, "It was modified by the amendments of the Senate Labor Committee after exhaustive hearings; it was further improved by amendments on the Senate floor last year; still further improved by re-drafting; and finally, following further hearings, perfected still further by 46 amendments and strengthened by the addition of Senator Javits and Cooper as co-sponsors.

"In short, Mr. President, the bill which is before the

Senate today is a most carefully drafted and effective piece of legislation. It is a bipartisan bill on a non-partisan subject. It covers all the outstanding recommendations of the Mc-Clellan Committee."

Goldwater's back stiffened and straightened at this. He looked around the chamber. Was there no one, no single member of that body, who had penetrated the sophistry of this statement?

"—Including provisions to assure full reporting of union financial and administrative practices, standards and procedures for the count of secret union elections, standards and procedures for the imposition of trusteeships upon subordinate bodies by national and international unions, controls on the activities of management and middlemen, and provisions to eliminate the no-man's land in labor-management relations."

Goldwater turned his eyes to the galleries. Most of the visitors would not have read the bill; only a few had any notion of the issues involved.

The crew-cut Senator from Massachusetts was glib and persuasive. He brought to his task a boyish atmosphere of sincerity. It almost appeared that he had already won his victory.

"In its present form," Kennedy continued, "as reported by the Committee, this bill represents a sound basis for obtaining effective labor reform legislation this year." With that bold claim, the Senator from Massachusetts requested permission to insert a point-by-point analysis of the bill as prepared by the majority of the Committee. This accomplished, he requested the privilege of the floor for Professor Archibald Cox of the Harvard Law School, chairman of the so-called Blue Ribbon Committee.

Now there was time to kill before rules for the debate were established. So the Senator from Massachusetts introduced a statement by twenty-one college professors recommending the need for strengthening the national responsibility for unemployment insurance on a permanent basis, and he followed this with an attack on the loyalty oath which had been included over his objections in the National Defense Education Act.

The Majority Leader suggested that six hours limitation be imposed upon debates—that debates be commenced after the morning hour on the following Monday.

There were the usual courteous inquiries to clarify the suggested time allocations and the session droned on to its desultory conclusion.

In the days that followed, the Record was filled with attempts at amendment, angry statements from newspaper editors, and an endless discussion of the exact meaning of the language of the voluminous legislation.

As time was finally running out on April 25, Goldwater of Arizona, who had led the attack on the inadequacies of the proposed Senate bill, claimed the floor.

"Mr. President, for more than two years the McClellan Committee has revealed almost daily, to the horrified gaze of the public, a shocking picture of corruption, racketeering and dictatorship in some segments of the labor-management field, and a high potential for misconduct in many of those areas which are still uncorrupted.

"The American public demanded effective measures to halt these dangerous conditions and trends and the U.S. Senate proceeded to develop legislation. It labored long and mightily, and like the proverbial mountain it brought forth the proverbial mouse. Although, Mr. President, I will say this mouse has today a great deal more muscle than when it was born.

"The bill, as now developed by this body in terms of its effect on evil conditions it professes to cure, is like a flea bite to a bull elephant.

"It not only omits provisions for the slightest additional control of the flagrant evils of secondary boycott, but in many of its provisions it does not accomplish what it gives the appearance of seeking to do. Even if unintended, the end result of this bill in its present form will be to mislead the American public into the false belief that adequate measures have been adopted to cope with the evils they abhor.

"Mr. President, I do not choose to be a party to this deception. I shall vote against the bill, and I shall regard it as my duty, not only as a Senator, but also as an American citizen to utilize every possible opportunity to enlighten the public about how they've been deceived."

The presiding officer called for the question—shall it pass? Yeas and nays were ordered and the clerk was instructed to call the roll.

Those Senators absent were announced. In some instances, their support of the bill was noted.

From Aiken of Vermont to Young of Ohio the responses were recorded: 90 yeas; 1 nay—Barry Goldwater of Arizona.

CHAPTER II

# NINETY-FIVE TO TWO

THE PASSAGE of the Kennedy-Ervin Bill in the Senate had been a foregone conclusion, but the overwhelming acceptance of this bit of political hypocrisy had not been anticipated by the Senator from Arizona. Goldwater, the lone dissenter, was fully aware of the enormity of his defeat.

The liberal press stepped up its attacks—did the dashing jet pilot from Arizona really believe that ninety members of the Senate were out of step and he was the only member of that body with sufficient intelligence or sufficient determination to serve the best interest of America? Or was he just a labor-hater with an overwhelming ambition to destroy the union movement by unnecessary and restrictive Federal legislation?

Some of the Senator's colleagues on the labor committee privately admitted the Kennedy-Ervin Bill did not satisfy all their desires, but why butt your head against a stone wall? Both the labor union lobbyists and the great apparatus of

academic liberalism had been effectively mobilized to support Kennedy's proposal. Maybe next year an amendment
or two might be had, but nothing more could be done now.

In the House of Representatives, there seemed little likelihood that either the administration-sponsored bill or the
adequate Landrum-Griffin proposal could win sufficient support for passage. The best to be hoped for was House con-
currence in the general provisions of the Kennedy-Ervin
legislation.

Lobbyists for the unions were using the nearly unanimous
vote in the Senate as leverage to tighten the screws of their
control on members of the House.

In Senator Goldwater's home state the labor unions were
not guilty of gross bad practice. In fact, Arizona had been
singularly free of labor disputes, such as those which have
marred many industrial communities of the nation. Because
his state was not directly involved, Goldwater found himself
the target of critics who pretended to find some ulterior
motive in his acceptance of the leadership of those in opposition to the many gross abuses of the labor movement
unchallenged by the Senate bill. A man of lesser determination might have accepted the inevitable and elected to
permit the matter to drop.

But requests poured into his office from all over the nation
for copies of his Senate statement condemning the weakness
of the Kennedy-Ervin Bill. He turned his speaking engage-
ments into a forum for repeating and documenting his con-
demnation of the proposed law which, in his words, "would
not correct the abuses disclosed by the McClellan Committee and didn't live up to the promises in its high sounding
title or the merits ascribed to the legislation by Kennedy of
Massachusetts."

Goldwater had walked out of the Senate Chambers on the night of the vote a lonely minority of one. He had been out-voted, but he was not yet ready to surrender.

It was in this frame of mind that Barry Goldwater attended a policy breakfast at the White House. The sun-tanned Chief Executive relied on these regular get togethers with Republican leaders of the Senate and House to provide him with an understanding of legislative problems. When it came time to discuss the recent Senate passage of the Kennedy-Ervin Bill, Ike turned to the Senator from Arizona and asked for an explanation of that notable, lone, dissenting vote.

Goldwater, who has great respect for Eisenhower as an individual and who has never been intimidated in the Presence, replied promptly and directly.

"This bill, Mr. President, does not deal with nor curb blackmail picketing or secondary boycotting. It ignores the no-man's land and fails to protect union members in their right to have a voice in the affairs of the union's operation. Its provisions for correcting the fiscal abuses practiced by some unions are woefully inadequate."

The Junior Senator from Arizona who had lived and suffered through the hearings, who had read and re-read every phrase of the Kennedy-Ervin Bill anxiously seeking to find some merit, rapidly documented his charges, item by item, provision by provision, until the President, with one of his infectious grins, called a halt.

"If I had been with you as a member of the Senate," Ike said, "I would have voted as you did."

The conversation ended. Despite the President's frank endorsement of Barry's opposition to the inadequacies of the bill, there was no indication of any action. The President's Secretary of Labor had sent a message to the Senate asking for stricter regulation and apparently the administration was satisfied with the bill as amended.

The brothers Kennedy throughout the McClellan hearings had very carefully highlighted the hoodlum acts of the Teamsters. By thus concentrating upon Jimmy Hoffa, public attention and understanding had been successfully diverted from what Goldwater regarded as the more dangerously evil practices of the few union dictators who had perverted the legitimate labor union movement into a weapon to destroy individual rights and freedoms.

Brutality on the picket line, threats of violence against employers, the use of gangland methods to collect heavy tribute from both workers and management as the price of labor peace, the looting of union treasuries by the Becks and Dios—all of these were, to Goldwater's way of thinking, only the most conspicuous evidence of the wounds being inflicted upon the nation by irresponsible labor leaders.

In Wayne County, Michigan, union muscle men, paid out of the AFL-CIO political funds, had taken over the Democrat Party machinery.* In dozens of other areas, union funds had been used to corrupt elections and to purchase victory for political candidates who would be subservient to the demands of union leaders.**

---

* "The CIO and the Democratic Party," by Fay Calkins, University of Chicago Press, page 118, page 121, page 123: "The 1950 State Democratic Convention. Most of the old guard defeated at the district conventions decided to boycott the state party convention. George Fitzgerald announced that he refused to attend a convention the delegates to which had been picked with 'storm troopers guarding the doors and the chairman presiding with a baseball bat.'" (Detroit News, September 27, 1950).

** Honorable Ralph W. Gwinn of New York in the U.S. House of Representatives, Monday, March 24, 1958, said: "Let's look at just 1 campaign, in 1954, by 1 union, for 1 Senator. Special election radio and TV broadcasts cost for time only, with no allowance for staff, script preparation, reprints of

Goldwater, to a much greater extent than his critics credited him, was aware that in many instances backward and selfish management policies had made it necessary for labor to organize. He believed, without any qualification, that free men should have the right to join freely any organization they regard as desirable in order to accomplish any lawful purpose. It is when compulsion enters the picture that Goldwater rebels, and it was the brutal compulsion of blackmail picketing and the secondary boycott, plus his understanding of the desperate helplessness of small business, and groups of laboring men caught in the "no-man's land" between federal and state laws which inspired Goldwater's determined opposition to the feeble provisions of the Kennedy-Ervin Bill.

Following his brief conversation with Goldwater at the White House, Eisenhower ordered his staff to make a careful analysis of the Kennedy-Ervin Bill, and then to make inquiries of the House leadership regarding the prospects for some improved legislation from that body.

At 7:30 PM Eastern Daylight Time on August 6, 1959, the President spoke to the nation. There was somber seriousness in the President's manner as he smiled at the TV camera. His opening words were these:

"I want to speak to you tonight about an issue of great importance to every man, every woman, and every child in this nation. It is above any partisan political consideration.

---

talks, was $250,000. Special election editions of regular publications, extra copies to distribute outside the regular union membership ran to another $175,000. And then, on top of all this, this union hired 500 'special organizers' (payroll title for political workers) at $20 per day for the 30 days just before the election. This cost another $300,000, exclusive of expenses or other services. This gives us a total of $725,000 spent by the United Automobile Workers, CIO, in support of Senator McNamara in Michigan in 1954."

It affects every American regardless of occupation, regardless of political affiliation.

"I speak of labor reform legislation.

"This nation," the President said, "needs a law to meet the kind of racketeering, corruption and abuses of power disclosed in many instances by the McClellan Committee." He called these revelations a "national disgrace" and he said:

"I want only effective protection from gangsters and crooks for the people of America—for the men and women who labor with their hands, their minds, their energies, to make America a better place for themselves and for their families."

After declaring his belief that the majority of employers, employees, and union bosses were above reproach, the President said: "To date legislation to correct these deplorable conditions has not been enacted." He could have been referring to the fact that no labor bills had passed the House; certainly there was an implication condemning the Senate action.

Then Ike outlined for all the nation to hear the root of the existing evils which had so long plagued the conscience of Goldwater.

"Take a company in the average American town—your town," said the President. "A union official comes into the office, presents the company with a proposed labor contract, and demands that the company either sign or be picketed. The company refuses, because its employees don't want to join that union. And remember, the law definitely gives employees the right to have or not to have a union.

"Now what happens? The union official carries out the threat and puts a picket line outside the plant—to drive away customers—to cut off deliveries. In short, to force the employees into a union they do not want. This is one example of what has been called blackmail picketing.

"I want that sort of thing stopped, so does America.

"Take another company," the President continued, "let us say a furniture manufacturer. The employees vote against joining a particular union. Instead of picketing the furniture plant itself, unscrupulous organizing officials, in this case, use another scheme. They picket the stores which sell the furniture this plant manufactures. The purpose is to prevent those stores from handling that furniture.

"How can anyone justify this kind of pressure against stores which are not involved in any dispute. They are innocent bystanders. This kind of action is designed . . . to force those employees into a union they do not want. This is an example of 'secondary boycott.'

"I want that sort of thing stopped, so does America."

In his 1500 word speech, the President outlined a sad dilemma: a small business, small union caught in the no-man's land between federal and state jurisdiction.

"Now let us examine what Congress has done so far this year."

Goldwater at his television set had not been provided with a copy of the President's speech. Would Ike give even tacit approval to the feeble Senate effort?

"Has its action measured up to the minimum requirements I have outlined to protect the American people? I regret to say that, as yet, the answer is no—definitely no.

"The bill which passed the Senate in April is not effective. It does not deal with or curb the picketing or boycotting practices I have described. And while it purports to deal with the 'No-Man's Land,' it gives no real relief.

"In the House of Representatives, the Labor Committee

bill is even less effective than the Senate bill. It, too, fails
to deal with picketing and boycotting practices I have described. Its provisions relating to the 'No-Man's Land' go
precisely in the wrong direction. And it actually exempts
about 70% of all unions from reporting on their finances. It
even removes criminal penalties against those who violate
the rights of union members.

"Neither the Senate bill nor the House Committee bill will
really curb the abuses the American people want to see
corrected."

Ike concluded with a statement that "Americans want
reform legislation which will be truly effective. It is my
earnest hope that Congress will be fully responsive to an
overwhelming national demand.

"Thank you and good night."

When the Chief Executive had finished, there were tears
in the Senator's eyes. His two years of effort; his having
endured the abuse, the sneering and condescending attitude
of the liberal press; had all been made worthwhile by the
blunt, direct words of the President of the United States.

For all practical purposes, Ike had voted with Goldwater.
The President had been in earnest that morning at the White
House; moreover, he had translated his convictions into
effective action.

What happened following that statement is history. In the
House the weak, inadequate companion piece to the Kennedy-Ervin Bill was defeated.

The Landrum-Griffin Bill, which promised a remedy for
the evils and yet protected legitimate labor unions, was
adopted by the House and sent to a conference committee.

The committee report came to the Senate. On September
3 the greatest deliberative legislative body in the world

reversed itself by a vote of 95 to 2, with only Senators Langer of North Dakota and Morse of Oregon in opposition. The Kennedy-Ervin Bill, conceived in hypocrisy, died an ignominious death. Truth and justice had triumphed. The Landrum-Griffin Act was signed into law by President Eisenhower.

No one has reported making an exhaustive search of the legislative history of the Congress to find a similar reversal of this proportion. Goldwater himself has made no such attempt. For him it is sufficient that the welfare of the nation has been served. He sometimes good-naturedly uses this experience as an example to encourage pessimists who profess to see no possible future for the Republic.

"When 1 to 95 in April becomes 95 to 2 in September," Goldwater says, "how can you doubt the vitality of representative government?

"It was more than the President's speech," says Goldwater. "It was, in fact, beyond the Congress. The American people demanded action. Hundreds of thousands of letters were sent to Washington, written by men and women whose lives were not involved as participants in labor-management disputes.

"The people won this one, not Goldwater," says the Senator with a grin.

# CHAPTER III

# IN SEARCH OF FREEDOM

**B**IG MIKE GOLDWATER renounced his allegiance to Emperor Alexander III of Russia on July 29, 1861, to become a citizen of the United States. Ninety-nine years later, one of Big Mike's grandsons was the sentimental favorite of the Republican Convention for the office of President of the United States.

Big Mike left his birthplace in the province of Posnan, Poland, and fled to England seeking freedom, a quest which finally brought him to the Mother Lode country of California and on to the frontier wilderness of Arizona.

Big Mike's grandson, Barry, went to the Chicago Convention hoping to convince his party it was time to halt the concentration of power in the federal establishment and restore responsibility and sovereignty to the individual citizen.

Mike Goldwater sought personal freedom—escape from

the tyranny of a government which denied equality to certain of its citizens, and a greater opportunity than was permitted by the class-conscious social system of the old world.

United States Senator Barry Goldwater, who loves this land and its people, whose perspective as a second generation American permits him to see, first of all, those things which are good and great in our society and our political institutions, entered the lists in Chicago to defend for all Americans the right to enjoy the opportunity which lured his grandfather across the ocean.

Life was never very easy for the patriarch of the Goldwater clan. He made no lucky strikes but there's no record of his having made complaint. It was sufficient to have escaped the chains that would have bound him had he stayed in the land of his birth.

Barry's maternal grandfather was Robert Royal Williams, a school teacher and farmer who settled first in western Illinois and moved later to Nebraska. Scotch, and militantly Protestant, this father of four daughters and two sons claimed to be a direct descendant of Roger Williams.

The latter half of the 19th Century was a period of revolutionary change. The physical limits of the world were being explored and expanded and the rigid economic and social structures were being swept aside by the industrial revolution. It was an age of misery and optimism. It was as Dickens said, "The worst of times, the best of times." Heroic exploits were commonplace. Immigrants by the tens of thousands crossed the ocean to the new world. Few of them brought less in the way of worldly goods or travelled farther than the grandfather of Arizona's Junior Senator. Tall, fair, with the same straight mouth and square jaw which has made it possible for the caricaturists of our time to sketch Barry with a few deft lines, Big Mike displayed the same qualities of leadership which have catapulted his grandson to such prominence in the politically troubled mid-years of the 20th Century.

That his friends and associates called him "Big" Mike is significant. He was blocky and well muscled, but not a giant of a man. His contemporaries used the term without particular reference to physical size. Mike was always looking ahead, taking the big view; he saw the best in each man who crossed his path, was trusting but not gullible. At one time in his early years in Arizona, Big Mike was financing many of the mercantile establishments north of the Gila River in a territory where the animosities of nature and depredations of Indians made any commercial venture extremely hazardous.

Big Mike travelled the lonely trails of Arizona; he encountered bandits, Indians on the war path, faithless friends and men out to ruin him. His forward progress was always the purposeful action of a man who knew where he was going. This same trait of character is causing Republicans to stamp their feet and cheer themselves hoarse when they learn of Senator Goldwater's blunt and simple belief in the worth and dignity of each individual.

Before Big Mike and his brother Joe Anglicized it, the name was Goldwasser. Hirsch and Elizabeth Goldwasser maintained an inn on the river bank in the city of Konin, west of Warsaw. Elizabeth Goldwasser gave birth to twenty-two children, and hard-pressed Hirsch never quite stayed even with his family's demands. There were too many mouths to be fed, too many bodies to be clothed, too many feet to be shod.

The lot of Jews in early 19th Century Russian Poland was

difficult. They were not permitted to attend universities or to become officers in the Czar's armies, or to earn their livelihood except by following restricted careers.

Jewish boys pressed into the military service were frequently forced to remain for most of their adult lives. There were restrictions on the ownership of land and educational barriers which forced the Jewish community into a scholasticism centered around Talmudic studies in their synagogues.

Wealthier families customarily sent their children to foreign countries, particularly to the German states, for higher education. But the majority of Jews lived and died in tight constricted family circles. Boy children became skilled tailors by the time they were ten or twelve, or worked as clerks and accountants in family businesses. To escape the military draft, Jewish boys often found some pretext to visit an uncle or cousin in another country.

Mike Goldwater's parents were too poor to send him abroad for an education. He learned to read and write at home, became acquainted with figures, and mastered the tailor's trade. Not unlike other victims of oppressive treatment, the Jewish people expressed their discontent by supporting, and in many cases leading, the frequent abortive attempts to win Poland's freedom from conqueror Russia.

It is difficult to believe that a fourteen year old boy, without formal education, who had never travelled more than ten miles beyond the place of his birth, could become much of a threat to the Emperor of all Russia. Whatever the nature of his offense against the government, it was sufficient to convince him there would be dire consequences if the Emperor's troops caught up with him.

Other members of the family told Sarah later that Big Mike would have faced a firing squad or been hanged had he

remained in Posnan. But there is no evidence that Hirsch
or Elizabeth suffered in any way from Mike's revolutionary
activity.

Whatever the nature or seriousness of his crime against
the Russian overlords, Mike Goldwater was a political fugitive before he reached his fifteenth birthday. He made his
way across the border into the German state ahead of his
pursuers. He never returned to Posnan. He never saw Elizabeth or Hirsch again. He never discussed the episode with
any of his children. It is in some ways a most revealing insight into this man who never looked backward once during
his long lifetime that he regarded the fact that he was forced
to flee from his father's homeland as relatively unimportant.

The attitude of the German government toward Jews was
more tolerant, but Big Mike wanted to put greater distance
between himself and his Russian pursuers and he felt there
was more opportunity in Paris.

Under the regime of Louis Phillippe, the middle class was
emerging as a strong identifiable element in French life.
No longer were there only two classes—the very, very poor
and the very, very rich. Between poverty and privilege there
was developing a middle class—the well-educated and mod-
erately prosperous bourgeoisie.

Paris was gay and attractive—Mike was young and willing.
There were customers aplenty for tailors who could satisfy
the demands of luxury-loving Parisians. In six months Mike
Goldwater mastered the language; he was a hard worker
and good craftsman. He also enjoyed the sudden freedom of
Paris night life. The boy from the provinces, alone and adrift
in a cosmopolitan city at an impressionable age, made friends
quickly. Having tasted the more open opportunities of

France, he eagerly questioned travellers regarding conditions in England and in the new world.

When the French government collapsed on February 24, 1848, turmoil and hardship descended on the city. Street fights, executions and deportations prodded Mike Goldwater into taking action he had long considered. This time he was no fugitive fleeing in the night. When he crossed the channel into England he took with him the modest capital he had acquired in eleven years of toil, and a degree of self-confidence far beyond his years.

Barry Goldwater never knew his grandfather. At first glance it would seem that the two men, separated by time and distance, had little in common beyond their name. Closer inspection reveals a number of striking parallels in their lives.

Big Mike met Sarah Nathan in London when he was twenty-six years old. Two years later they were married. Sarah told her children she determined on Mike as a husband the first day she laid eyes on him. The dominating qualities of Mike's character indicate this story was a happy fiction. Most Jewish boys of that period married young. Mike had remained single until he could establish his economic independence.

Barry met Margaret Johnson when her mother brought her into the Goldwater store in Phoenix and introduced her to the most eligible bachelor in town, with a suggestion that her daughter was finding life among strangers in this winter resort a dull experience. Two years later Barry and Margaret were married.

Mike Goldwater was the tallest of his father's sons and Barry is a full head taller than was his father, Baron.

Mike, throughout his lifetime, was more adventurer than business man. Family records suggest he was never able to give his undivided attention to any single enterprise. His grandson, who left college in the depression years to take over the family store following his father's death, has never been able to give his single-minded attention to any one business pursuit. Both men exhibited a restlessness in their early years.

Big Mike, although a merchant, frequently worked with his hands and enjoyed physical labor.

Barry, at those infrequent times when he is home in Arizona, will usually be found in an old pair of khaki pants and a T-shirt performing a variety of physical chores around his hilltop home. In December, 1960, when his emergence as a national political figure following the Nixon campaign was producing dozens of pleading requests for his appearance, Barry spent all of one day digging a hole through his black top driveway and erecting a flag pole.

Big Mike was a man of action. He strode forward to meet each new day with a warm embrace. His eyes were constantly on the far horizon. With it all he was an extremely practical man. His contemporaries said, "Big Mike never made the same mistake twice." Grandson Barry, Colorado River explorer, photographer, jet pilot, radio ham, is truly a 20th Century reflection of his 19th Century grandfather.

The differences between these two are primarily the result of a changing society.

Big Mike was a builder, restless to solve new problems. Cut off by circumstances from the land of his birth, he was never identified statically with any single geographical location. He kept expanding and enlarging. Barry, whose family's history in America parallels the history of Arizona, has always felt himself to be intimately related to the development of his state.

Big Mike, who fathered seven children, was separated from his family, except for brief moments, the first twenty-seven years of his marriage. The western mining camps where Big Mike was carving out a fortune were not a proper place for Sarah and the youngsters. Mike might have been willing to take them but Sarah flatly refused, and with the exception of the first few years of their life together in the new world, Mike maintained his wife and family in either Los Angeles or San Francisco. Sarah preferred the larger city to the north and Mike indulged her, but, for all the distance and difficulty of travel, the feeling of family unity and affection was never stronger than that between Sarah and Mike and their sons and daughters.

Barry, who seems to be constantly crossing the continent, whose wife and four children have never been in Washington with him more than a few weeks at a time, is actually closer in many ways to his children than most fathers who are not physically separated from their families.

Michael Goldwater and Sarah Nathan were married in London on March 6, 1850. Mike was twenty-eight years old and gave his occupation as tailor; Sarah was twenty-six and listed herself as a seamstress. She had, in fact, been supporting her family at her trade since her father's death some six years earlier. The marriage ceremony was performed in a synagogue by a rabbi who was a long-time friend of the Nathan family. Sarah's sister, Esther, didn't think much of the marriage, and in later years this initial disapproval expressed itself in a violent antagonism toward Mike's younger brother, Joseph.

At twenty-one, Joseph fled Poland to escape being drafted into the Russian conscript army. He came to London in 1851 where Mike and Sarah took him in.

The contrast between the two brothers was remarkable. Joe was small, swarthy, difficult to know, and always ready to make a change. His elder brother was tall, big boned, fair, a ready mixer, instantly liked, predictable and steady.

It was Joe who talked Mike into the great adventure. From members of the Jewish community and from reading the English newspapers which he soon mastered, Joe became infected with gold fever. News of the fabulous discoveries at Sutter's Mill had spread across the North American continent and across the Atlantic Ocean.

"I've talked with our countrymen who have come back from there," Joe told his brother. "Anyone can seek the gold. It belongs to those who find it. Anyone can start a business. The miners are eager to buy."

"What of Sarah and the children?" Mike countered.

"They can come later. We can be merchants. You couldn't do this in France. You haven't been able to do it in London. Do you want to be a tailor all your life and sit cross-legged on the floor working with a needle until you are so blind you stick your finger with every stitch?"

Mike Goldwater didn't want to be a tailor all his life. Neither was he willing to accept Joe's current enthusiasm as solid fact. He and Sarah discussed the matter. Mike made it a point to speak with others who had firsthand knowledge of the opportunities in America.

"It is true," they said. "Any man who can buy a stock of goods can go into business for himself. There are no pogroms against the Jews." There was, in fact, very little of the old world animosity toward them. It is very probable this tolerance was the deciding factor which took Mike and Joe Goldwater to the London docks in the spring of 1852. Sarah and the two children, Caroline and Morris, would stay in

England and Sarah would provide for herself and the children at the seamstress' trade.

San Francisco in November of that year was infected with "get rich quick fever." Every aspect of the city was stained with the color of gold. Men gambled their lives to find it and the once quiet, cultured city by the Golden Gate played any tune which would suit the miners' pleasure.

Joe and Mike, having come this far, had no intention of bucking the competition of established enterprises in the city. They spent several weeks listening eagerly to the reports from the gold camps, and finally settled on Sonora, one of the newest of the diggings in the foothills of the Sierras.

When Dooley's stagecoach deposited them on the main street of the mining camp of Sonora, Mike and Joe had in mind opening a general merchandise establishment. Within a week they gave up this idea. There were several general stores in town. Their meager capital would not permit them to acquire a stock adequate to challenge the established merchants; instead, they opened a saloon in a downstairs location beneath the town's most popular bordello. The bar was made of rough pine planks. There was no mirror, no stools, and only a few tables.

In later years, when Prohibition caused all the saloons in America to go underground, Big Mike's son, Baron, the father of Senator Barry, had a length of brass rail transferred from his favorite saloon to a bar in the basement of his North Central Avenue home in Phoenix. Baron and his friends drank their highballs and cocktails with their feet on the polished rail confronting a handsome mahogany bar with mirrored back and fancy crystal.

The early establishment of Big Mike Goldwater and his brother Joe was fantastically crude by comparison, but busi-

ness was good. Big Mike made friends readily and the
added attraction of the upstairs establishment was like a
built-in guaranty of prosperity.

The brothers slept on cots at the rear of the saloon. Day-
times they explored other commercial possibilities; at night,
they served the customers.

The morals of a western mining camp might be shocking
by today's standards; there was gambling, drinking, prostitu-
tion, and little else to compensate for the hardships encountered. With it there was a friendliness for strangers, a no-
questions-asked welcome and a strict code of honesty. Sonora
was crude and vulgar and incredibly primitive, but the
pilgrims from Posnan were made welcome by Jew and Gentile alike. They worked hard and minded their own business.
In fifteen months Mike had saved enough money to pay the
passage for Sarah and their two children and to finance the
passage for Sarah's recently widowed sister, Esther.

On July 2, 1854, Big Mike was reunited with his wife and
children in San Francisco. Sarah, who had never been out
of London, found much to dislike in the new world, but the
old ties had been cut and there was nothing to go back to.
His wife may have been homesick, but Big Mike never
looked over his shoulder.

CHAPTER IV

# M. GOLDWATER AND BROS.
# OF ARIZONA TERRITORY

THE GOLDWATER name came to Arizona from California in 1860 in a peddler's wagon drawn by two bay horses. Big Mike was on the driver's seat. The wagon was loaded with Yankee notions. To reach his destination—the new mining camps east of the Colorado and north of the Gila Rivers— Mike left Los Angeles and travelled alone across two hundred miles of desert, ferried the Colorado at Yuma and entered a hostile land where there were few roads and fewer people.

Arizona was still a part of the territory of New Mexico. Apache Indians, the greatest fighting men ever to do battle on the North American continent, were determined to keep the white man out of their homeland. But gold had been found and the lure of the precious metal outweighed the menace of hostile Indians, blistering desert sun, and the trackless wilderness.

We who live in the age of the motor car and the airplane can never truly understand the hardships nor appreciate the quiet courage of the men and women who pioneered the West. A thousand "Westerns" have added to our ignorance. The brutal finality of the climactic ten-second gun fight; the swift raid on the wagon train; the howling savages and flaming arrows; actors pitiously begging for water—all are transitory, all concentrated in minutes, or at the most—hours.

Men were not tried by crises in the true West. There was little of the release afforded in the dramatic showdown. Instead, death was a lurking shadow beyond the trees, on the horizon, in the grass of the meadow. Always there, always relentless, demanding the kind of enduring courage more often expressed by persistence in the face of almost certain failure than in the speed of a draw.

It is doubtful that Big Mike Goldwater ever thought of himself in heroic proportions. There were profits to be made in the mining camps, and the desire to succeed and become independent outweighed every other consideration.

The memory of defeat rode with Mike on the wagon seat. The years in Sonora, which started with such promise, had ended in failure. Sarah and her sister, Esther, had made no attempt to conceal their animosity for Joe. This family opposition broke up the original partnership and was perhaps the prelude to disaster.

During the first six months of Sarah's residence in Sonora there were twelve murders, and while Mike could accept the raw brutality of the town and be unaffected, Sarah's life was filled with discontent.

Joe tried other camps for a time and then returned to

Sonora and, financed by Mike, opened a second saloon which closed when Joe could no longer pay his bills and fled to escape his creditors. Business in general had not been good that year and Mike, feeling obligated to pay off his brother's debts, could ill-afford the capital loss.

Sarah, who was pregnant again, had already given birth to two children—Elizabeth and Samuel—in Sonora. Now she became determined to return to San Francisco and return she did with her sister and the four youngsters.

The financial strain of maintaining two establishments, coupled with the declining prosperity in the mining camp, posed a serious problem. Joe had gone to Los Angeles in 1858 and his letters were full of optimism. Shortly after the third Goldwater son, Henry, was born, creditors closed Mike Goldwater's Sonora establishment.

It is interesting to note that in both of these business failures there was no thought of bankruptcy. That portion of the debt which was not recovered from a liquidation of assets was ultimately paid out of Mike's later success.

Joe Goldwater had established a tobacco and notions store in the Bella Union Hotel—the social landmark of Los Angeles. The name on the window was J. Goldwater, although it is evident that Big Mike had provided the initial capital. Late in 1858, Mike, accompanied by Sarah and the children and Sarah's sister, established residency in Los Angeles. For a time Mike worked with Joe. He also bought and sold supplies on commission and acted as agent for other merchants interested in making contacts with San Francisco wholesalers.

When travelers brought word to Los Angeles of the rich gold strike in west central Arizona, the Goldwater brothers were eager to take advantage of the promised opportunity.

It is probable that Mike carried a keg or two of spirits along with the calico, notions, utensils and clothing which comprised the first Goldwater merchandise offered for sale in what is now Arizona.

It is not difficult to understand why Mike preferred the challenge of the mining camps to trade in the comfortable but unprogressive city of Los Angeles. In the new diggings, notions, utensils and clothing were more difficult to come by than gold, and almost as high priced.

Big Mike's grandson, Barry, accepted a similar challenge in the early days of World War II. German U-Boats had all but cut off the delivery of war materiel to America's allies in Europe, and the Air Force was driven to a desperate decision. Multi-engined aircraft were regularly being delivered by ferry pilots on the North Atlantic routes, but bombers couldn't function without fighter cover. Somehow single-engine fighters had to reach the theatre of war.

Captain Barry Goldwater had been participating in a project to determine the maximum range of the big Thunderbolt P-47s. On several occasions Goldwater had kept this single-engine plane in the air for nine and a half hours, covering non-stop a distance of more than eighteen hundred miles. When the Air Force called for volunteers in August of 1943, Barry and nine others eagerly accepted the opportunity to ferry the pursuit planes across the Atlantic.

Captain Goldwater in the cockpit of that P-47 gambled his life on the engine, navigation instruments, and the correctness of weather information. There was no margin for error. The thirsty radial engine drank fuel at such a rate that a miscalculation of one hundred miles would be likely to end in disaster.

To Barry Goldwater, too old for combat duty, freedom was

hanging in the balance and life was worth gambling to keep men free.

The journey of his peddler grandfather across the waste and wilderness eighty-two years earlier is perhaps, in our eyes, lacking the sharply edged drama of that over-the-water flight in an aircraft poorly equipped for the task. But the man in the cockpit and the man on the wagon seat were of the same breed—driven by the same irresistible motivation. They both knew the odds against success. Neither one was reckless, but the prize was worth the risk.

In the fifteen years between 1860 and 1875, Mike, at times alone, at times in partnership with others, developed a trade in Arizona which paralleled the rapid growth of the new territory. The original base of operations was La Paz, a mining camp on the eastern bank of the Colorado, midway between Fort Yuma and Needles. River steamers made the tortuous, dangerous journey from the mouth of the Colorado to a point one hundred miles upstream above La Paz. They brought merchandise of every description, from square pianos to surgical supplies.

When the disadvantages of the location at La Paz became obvious and the camp lost the county seat to Yuma, Mike built a whole new town and named it Ehrenberg, in honor of a German mining engineer who had become his closest friend in this wilderness outpost. From this base of operations as a wholesaler, Mike financed a large percentage of the territory's merchandising efforts.

There was money to be made in freighting. Army posts located at great distances had to be supplied with food for men and animals. Mike, in partnership with Dr. W. W. Jones, established the largest and best-equipped early transport service in the territory. It took fourteen days to make the journey from Ehrenberg to the territorial capital of Prescott. Supplies were hauled from the docks on the Colorado to such military outposts as Fort McDowell, on the Verde River, a journey requiring as much as a month. Millions of pounds of military goods were required and, with freight charges of three to four cents per pound per one hundred miles, the freighters could make a handsome return provided they didn't lose their "all" to the tortures of the trail or the menace of the Indians.

In discussing the family history, Barry has frequently said with some trace of chagrin:

"Mike made money from almost anything he did—trading, buying and selling mines, freighting, and always in the stores. Bob and I invariably lose money every time we tackle something outside our field."

In the early 1940's, Barry and his brother, Bob, financed an elaborate appliance center in Phoenix which ultimately folded. Immediately following the war Bob was the leading figure in the development of a local feeder airline which lost out to a more politically astute operator who took over the infant airline routes.

The early account books of Big Mike's enterprises indicate Barry exaggerates when he says that everything his grandfather touched turned to money. The first Phoenix store, opened in 1872, was closed three years later. While the store was not a success, it did serve to introduce twenty year old Morris Goldwater, Mike's first son, into the territory.

When Barry's father, Baron, the seventh child of Mike and Sarah, became old enough to enter the family business, the Goldwater store had been established in Prescott.

By this time, Big Mike had returned to California to be

reunited with Sarah after twenty-seven years of almost constant separation.

Barry's grandmother, after that first sad experience in Sonora, had resolutely insisted on bringing up her children where they would have the advantages of city life, and although Baron was born in Los Angeles during Sarah's brief period of residency in that city, he spent his early youth in San Francisco. Joe Goldwater had established an office in San Francisco in 1867 and most of the supplies which they sold in Arizona were purchased through this office. It was natural that Sarah should prefer the cosmopolitan atmosphere and pleasant climate of the Bay Region. In the early years there was too much risk in bringing the family to Arizona; later Mike was constantly on the road between his business enterprises in Tucson, Phoenix, Yuma, Prescott, Ehrenberg, and the source of supplies in Santa Fe and San Francisco.

Today almost all the evidence of the early West has been obliterated. The wagon trails of the pioneers are now coated with asphalt and concrete. Their watering places are obscured by magnificent motels with separate swimming pools for the youngsters and adults. People are everywhere; even the contemporary student of early history finds difficulty in understanding the lonely struggles which were commonplace one hundred years ago.

When Joe and Mike Goldwater moved to Los Angeles there were less than five thousand permanent residents in the old Spanish city. When Mike Goldwater came to Arizona, there were less than five thousand non-Indians in the entire territory—a land area equal in size to six or seven of the thirteen original colonies. There was no regular mail service, no effective civil government. Nowhere in history can we find a better insight into the make up and character of that polyglot racial mixture we call Americans than by a review of our westward expansion.

A middle-aged Jewish peddler on the seat of a spring wagon heading East through the mountain passes and across the desert to find customers for his goods—a fugitive from the ghettos of Poland, a tailor in Paris sewing on the finery of the nobility, a failure in his first business venture in the mining camp of Sonora—what did this man know of desert trails? Wagons break down and must be mended; horses grow lame and must be doctored; the threat of death from starvation or thirst is constant. Mile followed mile of palo verde and ocotillo. Water holes were widely separated and the supply was uncertain. Food for men and animals had to be carried.

From our comfortable vantage point today, with our engineering and mechanical ability, we constantly contend that anything is possible. Give us a problem, we marshal our resources, recruit personnel especially equipped by training and experience, and then move forward.

In the 19th Century West there was no place for a man to learn to live without water except by doing it. There were no schools to impart the skills needed to read correctly the desert land marks. Uncompromising nature was the instructor; the reward for a successful student was another day of life. The prize to be earned was nothing more than the right to continue the struggle, to depend upon your own resources, to be the architect of your own destiny; to live or die on your own, to be free.

Mike and Joe Goldwater, their sons and nephews traveled thousands of miles by freight wagon, buggy and horseback through Arizona at a time when such commanders as Generals George A. Stoneman, Orlando B. Wilcox, August Valentine Kautz, and George Crook were losing their battles to subdue the Apaches. A number of their early-day friends and partners were murdered by the Indians.* Joe and Mike and Mike's freighting partner Jones, travelling in two buckboards from Prescott to Ehrenberg on June 15, 1872, were attacked by a band of thirty renegades. Joe received two balls in the middle of his back. Mike was nicked. Despite their wounds, they outdistanced the Indians and fought them off.

Joe was taken to a Skull Valley ranch where Dr. Jones removed the two rifle balls and gave them to him for a present. He wore the balls on his watch chain for the remainder of his life. When he died a peaceful death at the end of a long and productive life, the family buried the balls with Joe, but this was thirty years after they were meant to kill him.

The emergence of Big Mike as the sole owner of the store in Ehrenberg and as entrepreneur in half a dozen other commercial establishments scattered across the frontier, has become one of the early legends of the territory.

Heinrich Heinsel, a German refugee who changed his name to Henry Wickenburg upon his arrival in America, discovered one of the fabulous gold mines in south central Arizona in November, 1862. He named it the Vulture.

Wickenburg formed a partnership with some San Fran-

---

* Herman Ehrenberg, Mike's good friend, was killed under mysterious circumstances. In the original manuscript, the writer joined some substantial authorities on Arizona history and attributed Ehrenberg's death to Indians. Barry, in his corrections, suggested this might not be true. Along with other students of history, he believes Ehrenberg was murdered for profit by the owner of a lodging house whose first name and origin has long been lost in the dim pages of the past. He was referred to by his contemporaries as "Double Assed Smith."

cisco backers and developed the prospect until he blocked
out sufficient ore to indicate the value of his find.

Who was there in the new territory of Arizona to finance
a stamp mill for the new mine? Mike Goldwater, of course,
and Wickenburg travelled to Ehrenberg, more than one hundred miles across the desert to seek Mike's assistance.

The two men were acquainted and Mike Goldwater, the
merchant, had up-to-date information on every likely gold
prospect in the territory. The deal was made. Mike would
find and buy a stamp mill and ultimately be paid with gold
from the prospect.

Mike wrote Joe, living in San Francisco, and suggested
that his brother select and purchase a suitable piece of mining machinery. Joe's answer indicates he had learned caution
from his failure in Sonora and his mediocre success in Los
Angeles.

"I'm a good judge of wine, expert on tobacco, and I'm
learning something about the general dry goods business,"
Joe replied, "but when it comes to gold machinery, I'm innocent of all knowledge."

Mike had no firsthand experience with mining machinery,
but he went to San Francisco and entered negotiations for
the purchase of the mill.

Big Mike had known nothing about wagons or horses or
Indians or the desert when he came to Arizona. The fact
that he'd never seen a stamp mill, much less operated one,
didn't stop him. After carefully inspecting all the machinery
offered, he purchased a huge twenty-stamp mill, a steam
engine boiler, and the necessary additional machinery, and
arranged for the lot to be transported on a coastal vessel to
the mouth of the Colorado River. The equipment was then
transshipped on a river boat to Ehrenberg where Mike Gold-

water's freight outfit transported it overland to a flat beside the Hassayampa River, a mile north of the present city of Wickenburg.

At that point in his business career, Mike was in partnership with a young man from Los Angeles named B. Cohn. When the mill had been in operation for some one hundred days, the books still showed no payments had been made to the firm of Goldwater and Cohn. The total indebtedness amounted to almost $35,000. The figure did not represent a complete loss, however, since the merchants had been supplying, on an almost exclusive basis, all the needs of the miners employed at the Vulture.

Big Mike made a trip to Wickenburg and before he left the mining company signed over its title to the Vulture as security for the debt, named Mike trustee and authorized him to operate both mine and mill until full payment was made.

The operation of a stamp mill was just another business. Mike stayed at the mill and ninety days later, after paying all expenses of operation, he had recovered almost $35,000 in gold. With the money on hand to liquidate the mining firm's obligations, Mike promptly returned the property to its original owners.

Cohn was anxious to sell his half interest in the Arizona operation. He offered to take the $35,000 in gold, which belonged to the partnership, in settlement for all his interest in the store at Ehrenberg and the other ventures which had been a joint effort. Big Mike was on his own at last.

Some seventy years later, Mike's grandson, Barry, took over a summer hotel for a season for exactly the same reason —to liquidate indebtedness incurred by the hotel's owners to the Goldwater stores. And, like his grandfather, when the debt had been paid, Barry returned the property to the original operators.

It was inevitable that Mike would ultimately settle on Prescott, Arizona, as headquarters for his business. Prescott had begun as a mining camp, but by that time it was far more. There was no similarity between Prescott's pleasant pine clad hills and the sparse desert growth of the Colorado region of Ehrenberg and La Paz.

Prescott was the territorial capital, vying with Tucson for a position of paramount importance in the new territory. The climate was kind, with pleasant summers and mild winters. It was the logical supply center for cattlemen in the northern half of the territory, and commercially it was far more active and prominent than Tucson. It was Big Mike's kind of town—bawdy, boisterous, constantly flexing its muscles in the race for leadership, enhanced by the presence of a cavalry command post and by its position as the center of purchasing for army supplies. Mike and Joe opened the Prescott store in October 1876.

Baron Goldwater, who became the father of Arizona's Junior United States Senator, arrived in Prescott on October 31, 1882, from San Francisco. He was sixteen years old, educated, well-dressed, and prepared by a period of apprenticeship in the San Francisco office to take an active part in the Arizona store.

Morris and Baron's older brother, Henry, were then in command of the establishment Big Mike had started. The family ties were strong; they welcomed their "little brother," but they weren't ready to accept him as an equal in the family enterprise.

Baron, who was next to the smallest of Mike's four sons, acknowledged the fact that Morris and Henry had seniority.

His brothers were of the frontier. They criticized him for ordering his clothes from Wanamaker's and for using cologne, and for a host of other habits he had acquired living in the city.

Baron may have been a dude, but he was no dunce. He cheerfully accepted his duties as a clerk, lived modestly, made no complaint about his situation, and turned his attention to a careful analysis of Big Mike's business empire.

The frontier was changing; Baron was the first to recognize it. The limited merchandise lines which had been sufficient to satisfy the desires of the pioneers of a decade earlier would always be in demand, but there were people in the territory who could afford to indulge themselves in some luxury and Baron was ready to go after this trade.

After more than a year in Prescott, he returned to San Francisco to lay the foundation for a certain change which he felt would enhance the profits of the Arizona store and assure its continuing prosperity.

Baron's first independent business venture is remarkably prophetic of the merchandising concept which made and has kept Goldwater stores in Arizona the established leaders in items of merchandise, high in quality and high in price.

When Baron returned to Prescott, he brought with him a magnificent, expensive square piano which he promptly sold at a handsome profit. He advertised pianos in the *Prescott Journal Miner* and from the listing it would indicate this was an independent venture, apart from the established Goldwater store. In the next few months, Baron sold more than a dozen pianos, to become unquestionably the largest volume piano dealer in Arizona.

Henry and Morris were convinced. In addition to being

a good salesman, Baron had demonstrated a keen ability to recognize a market possibility they had overlooked.

In 1888 Baron enlisted in Company A of the territorial militia. He made friends as easily as Big Mike, although the two were totally different in appearance and background.

On his twenty-eighth birthday, Baron was made a full and equal partner with Morris and Henry, and soon Morris began seeking greater fields for his little brother's talents to conquer.

Both Prescott and Tucson had been outdistanced in growth by the farming community of Phoenix in the center of the Salt River Valley. The capital, which had been moved from Prescott to Tucson and back to Prescott again, was established in Phoenix on February 7, 1889. The importance of mining as an economic factor was gradually dwindling, and there was good reason to believe the future growth of the territory would be based on agricultural development.

Morris, a confirmed bachelor in his middle forties, was fond of Prescott. He was the recognized Democratic Party leader in the county and his influence extended throughout the territory. Prescott might not be growing as fast as Phoenix, but the store was doing well enough to satisfy Morris; he had no intention of leaving.

There is a family story that the three brothers played a game of cards; the winner to stay in Prescott, the loser to move to the valley. It is unlikely that a card game had anything to do with it. Henry was more interested in travel and adventure than merchandising, and Morris was firmly entrenched in Prescott. At any rate, in 1896 a branch of M. Goldwater and Brothers was reopened in Phoenix with Baron in charge.

Baron liked Phoenix and Phoenix liked Baron. The ladies

appreciated his taste in dry goods and dresses; they also appreciated his charm. He was considered a cosmopolitan gentleman of wide experience because of his frequent buying trips to New York where he purchased merchandise for both stores. With his San Francisco background, Baron was readily accepted and earnestly sought after by the more attractive young girls in a Phoenix which was just beginning to enjoy more than a pioneer existence.

# CHAPTER V

## JOSEPHINE WILLIAMS GOLDWATER—
## "MUN"

THE RAILROAD coach was crowded, dirty and hot. The horsehair seats with their faded velour upholstery seemed designed to heighten the discomfort of the journey. The wooden floor had been painted and re-painted in vain attempts to conceal the checking and cracking of the ancient material. There were frequent stops to take on water and fuel, and the steam whistle, which had bellowed so magnificently in the Chicago Station, was now reduced by the vastness of the Kansas prairie to a shrill, protesting scream.

The young girl, her thin body crumpled on the seat, her face pressed to the window glass, appeared oblivious of her surroundings. For all her youth, she seemed frail and helpless. Beneath the hat, which had been stylish in Chicago, rebellious blond curls ran down the nape of her neck to be lost beneath the high collar of the limp, but defiant, travelling dress.

On the rack overhead a shiny straw suitcase, innocent of travel weariness, revealed its owner's situation. The suitcase and the handbag, the too bright cheeks and lips, all had a story to tell. If she were mindful of this revelation, there was no indication of resentment to be read in the deep untroubled blue eyes.

She had boarded the train unaccompanied. No one saw her off or fussed over her departure. The conductor, a weather-beaten Yankee character who had surrendered everything but his defiant mustache to the humdrum inconvenience of railroading, took in her plight at a single glance. A "lunger" heading West. Probably some farm girl who had succumbed to the temptation of Chicago's bright lights, and become one more victim of the city's unpredictable winter weather.

The girl's youth and beauty, apparent inexperience and defenseless indifference had provoked one of the male passengers to make overtures before the train was out of the Chicago yards. The girl had put him in his place with a scornful smile and a few words, spoken so softly no one else on the coach overheard. After that, the conductor revised his earlier appraisal and concluded that whatever the state of her health she possessed a spirit more sturdy than her appearance.

At the turn of the century, hapless patients suspected of lung trouble were invariably advised by their physicians to go West for the cure. Cynical critics have suggested this common advice was prompted as much by the doctor's desire to be rid of a medical problem he couldn't understand as by any real belief that the western climate possessed curative powers.

It has been said that at this particular period half the population of Arizona had come West to die. Old timers love to tell the story of the Scotchman from Michigan, the Colonel from England and the Wall Street lawyer who travelled to Phoenix under a death sentence of tuberculosis. The Scotchman, now eighty-five and still alive, delights in telling his friends that after much discussion on the train trip, he and his companions decided it would be much more pleasant to die from over-drinking than to waste away from lung fever.

"You know, mon, the three of us stayed drunk the first nine months we were here. Then Jackie boy looked at the calendar one morning and advised us that, since we were supposed to be dead in three months, we were somehow six months past the deadline. We'd might better be making plans for living."

If Josephine Williams, the girl on the day coach, ever had any intention of coming West to die, she never indicated that such an eventuality was even considered. The beloved and pampered mother of Arizona's Senator Barry Goldwater, "Mun," as she is affectionately called, is now past eighty and still an active participant in every family clambake and crisis. Her elder son credits her with instilling in his youthful breast the fierce love of country and the unswerving devotion to the concepts of the Republic, which have contributed in large part to his becoming a symbol of leadership in the confused and perilous 1960s.

"When I was just a little guy, not more than four or five years old," he says, "my mother used to drive us, Carolyn, my brother Bob, and me, out the dusty road to the Indian School so that we might witness the lowering of the flag.

"Usually it was summer time. When we turned off Central Avenue to Indian School Road and headed east, the air was like the exhaust from an overheated engine. We didn't know enough to know it was hot, but she did, and she took us just the same. Three miles out and three miles back to stand in silent respect as the flag came down. There was a new star on the banner for Arizona. It was the flag of freedom—freedom which brought my grandfather to this land—freedom which made our life possible—and Mun wanted us to share her love and reverence for this symbol of man's outreach for the independence and responsibility God intended man to find."

The sick girl on the day coach had been told by doctors in Chicago she had tuberculosis. A less resolute or self-sufficient young lady might have gone to pieces when confronted with the terror which was little understood and regarded as almost fatal in 1903. But Josephine Williams was a trained nurse and had been on her own since she was sixteen. When the doctor said Arizona, she wrote her parents a kind fabrication:

"I'm going to travel out west to Arizona with a patient whose health requires that climate," she said. "It may be sometime before I write again, but don't worry. A nurse never has any trouble finding a job and I may decide to stay out there if I like what I see."

Josephine had been born in Illinois and reared in the sand hills of Nebraska. She was certainly no wide-eyed tenderfoot. Still it is doubtful if she was prepared for what was in store for her. Her train ticket took her as far as Ashfork; she was bound for Phoenix two hundred miles to the south; she had no intention of depleting her meager store of cash to purchase a ticket on the local.

Josephine Williams' brother was a railroad telegrapher;
she knew the jargon of the key rappers. The agent at Ashfork
made arrangements for Jo to ride the caboose to Phoenix.

The capital city of Arizona was distinguished by its dusty
streets, bordered with open ditches carrying water to trees
which had been planted by the early pioneers. The main
street was named in honor of the country's first president.
West of Central Avenue, the east and west dividing line, a
square block was given over to a plaza for the county buildings. In a corresponding location on the east, the city hall
and jail enjoyed a setting more magnificent than the buildings deserved. On East Washington Street, between First
and Second Streets, the dry goods store of M. Goldwater
and Brothers was the finest in the territory. It was a long
time after her arrival by caboose before Josephine Williams
was even aware of the merchant or the merchandise at that
East Washington location.

"Lungers" lived in tents out beyond the city where they
could benefit from the dry heat of the desert, and for a time
the girl from Chicago was a part of this colony of desperation.

"Mun never has told us how long she lived in the tent,"
Barry says, "but we think it wasn't any longer than the time
it took her to recover from that tiresome six-day ride in the
day coach."

In a town which owed much of its growth to its reputation
as a health center nurses were at a premium, and shortly
after arrival the Williams girl was asked to take special duty
at St. Joseph's Hospital. How this request jibed with the
supposition that she was a victim of tuberculosis, Jo has
never explained. At any rate, within three months the young
nurse from Chicago was doing special duty and earning the

respect of the few doctors optimistic enough to cast their lot in a sun-baked city of less than 10,000 population.

The old Adams Hotel was the center of social life. The city was feeling its oats. There was talk of a constitutional convention and possible statehood. Baron Goldwater was the city's most eligible bachelor. It was inevitable that in such a limited situation Baron and the young nurse from Illinois would become acquainted. Mun says it was over the yard goods counter in Goldwater's store.

"I didn't buy what he tried to sell me," she says, "it was too high priced. But he was nice to talk to, although a little fresh and quite conceited."

Josephine Williams was twenty-nine and Baron Goldwater forty-one when he proposed. Their courtship had kept the town talking for more than a year.

"I wasn't the prettiest girl in town by a long shot," Josephine says, "I wasn't the youngest or the wealthiest; in fact, I think Baron regarded me as a hard case because I didn't faint at his flattery."

When Josephine had accepted him, Baron invited her to come to the store and select her trousseau.

"I'll do no such thing," she told the man she had just promised to marry. "Until I'm Mrs. Goldwater I'll pay my own bills and buy my own clothes where I choose." Then she softened somewhat, "Not that I don't think you have the finest and handsomest in all the territory, Baron."

Mun delights in telling her children that the wedding dress didn't come from Goldwaters.

"I bought some red silk from Korricks because it was less expensive and I had a lady sew it up for me. I never intended to be bossed by anybody and I thought your father might as well know it. It was a pretty dress, but not as nice as the

ones he had in the store. He knew it and I knew it, but we
never said anything. He respected my independence and all
our life together we were that way."

Morris, who represented the only family either Baron or
Josephine had in the territory, insisted that the wedding be
held in Prescott; Baron made no objection. Until the store
in that mountain city was closed it was always regarded as
headquarters for the Goldwater mercantile operation in Arizona.

A snowstorm was raging when Baron and Jo reached the
former capital city. Morris, who was then Mayor, made
arrangements with the local Episcopal priest to perform the
ceremony. The church was opened, the vows were made
and the party adjourned to Morris Goldwater's boarding
house for a wedding supper. The next day, Baron and Jo left
for New York—a combined honeymoon and buying trip.

The newlyweds returned to Phoenix and to a predicted life
of luxury and ease. But if anyone suspected that Josephine
Williams would surrender her independence in marriage,
their suspicions were soon disproved.

The young couple moved into an apartment on the corner
of Central Avenue and McKinley to wait out the craftsmen
who were completely refurbishing a big house half a block
south. In this rented, comfortable, two-story brick residence
Barry and Bob were born—Barry on New Year's Day, 1909,
and Bob fifteen months later. Carolyn was born in Prescott,
in the home of Tom Campbell who was later to become
Governor of Arizona.

Most of his life in Arizona, Baron had been called "Barry"
by his friends and associates. Now with a boy baby chris-
tened with a shortened and less formal version of his father's

name, some difficulty developed in keeping the two identities
straight.

"Mun never had any trouble," Barry says, "she never spoke
to Dad in the same tone of voice she reserved for us youngsters. But when I was growing up I fought the idea of being
called 'Little Barry.'"

Josephine and Baron are remembered by their close
friends as an ideal married couple. Jo was a gracious hostess,
entertained beautifully, and gave the appearance of being
guided by her husband's every wish.

Big Mike's son inherited none of his interest in the out-of-
doors or aptitude for roughing it. Even today Barry remembers his father as the best dressed man he's ever known.

"When I was just six or seven, I can remember Dad coming home from the store in the middle of the afternoon to
change his shirt," Barry says. "He never learned to drive a
car, never performed any physical labor, if he could hire
someone to do the work for him."

According to Mun, Baron loved his children dearly, but
was always slightly intimidated by them.

"He wanted it quiet when he came home from the store
and I saw to it the kids were quiet," she says.

Listening to the Senator recount the stories of his childhood, it is obvious that his father was a city man, his mother
the iron-willed pioneer.

"It was Mun who took us camping," Barry recalls, "it was
Mun who taught us to shoot. It was Mun who led us into
the unexplored areas of Northern Arizona and instilled in us
a curiosity about everything that went on in nature."

After his marriage, Baron Goldwater's life changed very
little. He'd given up his bachelor quarters and moved into a
big house, but he continued his regular midday card games

with cronies at the Arizona Club, and friends of his bachelor days invariably stopped for a drink at the downstairs bar in the big house on North Central as they made their way home after work each evening.

It was in this bar that Baron installed the length of brass rail taken out of his favorite saloon when Prohibition spread its hypocritical hand of decorum across the nation. Mun still has the brass rail in the home she built on Manor Drive next to Barry and Peggy and across the street from Bob.

Baron apparently was an indulgent father, always coming home from New York buying trips with new games and toys, but Barry now says somewhat wistfully: "I never really knew my father. I respected him. I felt that he loved us all very dearly, but his world was the store, club and his adult companions. With Mun it was different. She shared every youthful escapade. I can't remember any time when Carolyn, Bob or I kept any secrets from Mun."

On her part, the Senator's mother, now past her eightieth birthday, says, "My children always told me the truth. That was enough to make me overlook their pranks and difficulties."

In Central Arizona, prior to the development of refrigeration, there was a general exodus the minute school closed. Every man who could afford it, and some who couldn't, arranged for their families to escape the torrid summertime temperatures, either on the south coast of California or in the higher northern elevations of Arizona.

Each year Mun packed her brood and two or three neighbor kids into a big Apperson touring car loaded with camping equipment, and headed for the Southern California beach.

In early years the trip took as long as five days, and when

a wooden plank road was finally completed from Yuma to Brawley, the coast-bound travelers cut a full day off their time and rejoiced at the convenience of "modern living."

Of her children, Mun says she believes Barry is most like Big Mike, while Bob favors his father Baron; Carolyn is a combination of all the wild Goldwaters and sedate Williams' who ever lived.

Her peculiar nickname, which she prefers to Jo or Josephine, was bestowed on her by Barry.

"We had a housekeeper named Angie, and Baron frequently called me 'Mumsie.' Little Barry, confused by the two principal women in his life, settled the matter by combining Mumsie and Angie into 'Mun.'"

Josephine Goldwater is not the kind of woman who surrenders her entire life to her children. She took up golf and became first women's champion of Phoenix, and later on, State champion. She rode horseback and encouraged the youngsters to ride. She was mistress of one of the most elaborate domestic establishments in the territory, but still found time to interest Barry in reading Gibbons' "Decline and Fall of the Roman Empire" before he was eight years old. She tried, but was never able to make a serious student out of her first born. "He loved mechanical things; tinkered with parts of radio sets when he should have been studying; and spent a great deal of energy developing elaborate practical jokes."

In those early years, before there was air conditioning of any kind, the entire population of Phoenix slept outdoors from late spring to early fall. Some families had large screen porches, others simply moved beds into the backyard. The Goldwaters occupied a downstairs back porch which crossed the entire rear of the Central Avenue residence. One Fourth

of July when the family was still in Phoenix, nine-year-old
Barry awakened with an itch to commemorate the nation's
independence.

Mun always slept with a revolver under her pillow. She
had never used it and there was no practical need for it to be
there. Barry found the gun and emptied it into the ceiling
overhead. The noise created quite a commotion at that hour
of the morning. Heads popped out of the E. J. Bennitt residence to the south. Mun, awakened by the noise, called her
neighbors to say it was just Barry celebrating the Fourth of
July. Her husband, shocked by the noise and somewhat
startled to see his nine-year-old boy with a smoking revolver
in hand, pretended he had not been affected by the unusual
action until the ceiling overhead began to drip whiskey. The
random shots had found an unfortunate target. Baron had
two kegs carefully stored on the second floor where he believed the summer heat would aid in the aging.

"It's a tough thing to get punished for an accident," Barry
says now. "There would have been no penalty for firing the
gun or making the noise or waking up the neighborhood, but
because I accidently spilled his booze, I caught it something
fierce."

The Goldwaters in that pioneer town lived in what was
described as opulent luxury. Josephine had help in the
kitchen and with the housework and there was a man of all
work who looked after the teams and carriages, at first, and
later took care of the cars. Baron apparently never denied
anything to his wife and children, although he once com-
plained when Josephine paid eighty dollars a month for a
summer rental at the beach that his wife had lost her mind
and bought a mansion in California.

There were dozens of men in Phoenix wealthier than

Baron Goldwater. Many of them amassed estates running into the millions. When Baron died, just in advance of the great depression in 1929-1930, he left less than $300,000 to his heirs. He never became a millionaire, but for most of the days of his life he indulged himself and those he loved. He generously supported numerous charities and when the bank, which had made him a director because they needed the prestige of the Goldwater name, went broke, Baron liquidated other investments to pay off the loss.

If Baron wasn't a millionaire, he lived like one and the same charge is now repeated about his son. Barry, who is extravagant in many things, is extremely careful and prudent about making investments and entering deals. The combination of Big Mike's indomitable determination, Josephine's iron-willed pioneer spirit, Baron's friendly generosity, are all preserved in the personality of Arizona's Junior Senator.

# CHAPTER VI

# "TO MAKE A HOME,
# TO HAVE A FAMILY"

THERE was great excitement in the big house on North Central Avenue on New Year's Day, 1909. In her practical and professional efficiency, Josephine had made all the arrangements far in advance of the actual date. When the interval between pains told her it was time, she informed her husband that he might call the doctor.

The whole idea of fatherhood was new and somewhat terrifying to Baron Goldwater, an attitude and state of mind he never quite conquered. He was forty-three years old when his first son was born. Josephine, who intuitively seemed to sense his moods and cater to them, had made the transition from bachelor life to husband an easy one. Fatherhood was more difficult for him to accept.

Baron was proud of his first born. It pleased him that Barry Goldwater had arrived on New Year's Day. When his second son, Robert, was born on the Fourth of July fifteen months later, Baron was far better prepared for the event—he had made that discovery so important and reassuring to all fathers. After childbirth, the gracious mercy of God gives to new mothers the marvelous ability to live a dual life. Josephine, recovering rapidly from her delivery, had picked up with ease and confidence the responsibilities attendant upon being wife to a gregarious husband in a socially active western town. At the same time, Baron recognized that his child was wrapped and protected in alert motherly love. To him it seemed his wife's thoughtfulness and tenderness had increased with the birth of their first child.

Looking backward, it now appears nature might have slipped and somehow made a mistake on names and dates. For Bob, the sober, industrious business man and younger brother, was born on the Fourth of July. Had things been reversed and Barry come into this world on the anniversary of the Declaration of Independence, those observers of the American political scene who recognize and commend the fierce patriotism of Arizona's younger Senator, might find something more significant in his birth date.

Josephine Williams had been a member of the Episcopal Church all her life. It was natural she should have her children baptised in her faith. The fact that her husband was Jewish and his parents members of the Orthodox faith had little importance on the frontier.

If Baron had any personal preference in the matter it had nothing to do with Jew or Gentile. Big Mike and Sarah were both dead, but from them Baron had inherited a strong and abiding trust in the Almighty. Marriage had come late in life for him, and above everything else he wanted his children to recognize that man is more than animal, his existence

more than happenstance; that if our years on earth are to
be meaningful, we must feel an individual responsibility toward our creator; we must accept and submit ourselves to
God's commandments.

Josephine took motherhood and family in stride. This is
why they had the big house; this is why she'd married Baron
—to make a home, to have a family, to participate in God's
intended purpose for his creation.

In later years, Barry Goldwater has frequently said, "We
all must pay rent for the space we occupy on this earth.
There is more to life than successful merchandising, or shooting the rapids, or flying an airplane or achieving what men
call success."

Carolyn, Baron's third child and only daughter, was born
in Prescott in 1913 on the day the liner Titanic was sunk,
while Josephine was completing a month-long visit in the
city which had been the birthplace of the family's commercial prominence.

Barry's childhood was a combination of indulgent luxury
and responsible hardship.

"When I was just five years old," he says, "Mun took all
of us, that is Bob, Carolyn, and me, camping in the back
country of Arizona for two weeks. It was my job to chop the
wood and build the fire, and if I didn't do it right I was tail-
end Charlie in the chow line.

"Mun was like a scoutmaster, choir leader and rich grandmother," he says. "We could get away with almost anything
if we told her the truth. In fact, it never occurred to any of
us to lie to her. If she didn't approve there was bound to be
punishment, but if we had lied, we would have lost her
respect."

Arizona became a state on Valentine's Day, 1912. The new

status changed the political complexion of the state, and instead of appointed Republican Governors the people elected George Wiley Paul Hunt, an outspoken, capable Democrat.

The Salt River Reclamation Project was completed in 1911, and now with an assured supply of irrigation water, the central valley's agricultural prosperity was guaranteed. Phoenix was still a city of less than 15,000 population. Most of the streets were unpaved and even in the downtown sections the sidewalks were shaded by gigantic cottonwoods.

A spurline railroad, the Maricopa and Eastern, connected with the mainline of the Southern Pacific at Maricopa Junction. In the northern and southern portions of the state copper mining and cattle raising were supporting a growing economy. Farmers in the Phoenix area were gradually switching from wheat and feed grains to citrus and other crops particularly suited to the mild winters and warm summers.

The stores generally reflected the prosperous conditions throughout the state. Uncle Morris was Vice President of the Constitutional Convention, President of the Twentieth Territorial Council and spokesman for the Jeffersonian Democrats. As a pioneer banker as well as merchant and politician, Morris wielded tremendous influence. He had friends in the banking world from coast to coast, and, with the possible exception of George Hunt, Morris was the most respected man in the state.

This son of Big Mike Goldwater was only five feet, five inches tall. In Phoenix he lived like a prince in a special suite at the Adams Hotel. His dress was fashionable, his habits fastidious and his carefully waxed mustache bristled with dignity and self-assurance.

Jeff Adams, a frontier cattleman and a contemporary of
Morris and Baron, once said in all seriousness that the Goldwaters were whiskey drinking, wild horse riders who just
couldn't be second best at anything. Since neither Morris
nor Baron were cowboys, or ever rode horses when there was
another method of transportation available, the old cattleman's description must be regarded as symbolic. Small men
physically, the brothers more than compensated for their
lack of physical stature by determination, brains and personal charm.

Big Mike, who had been beaten a half dozen times by
nature, the antagonisms of business and misplaced trust in
some of his partners, had by natural vigor, persistence and
determination established the Goldwater habit of winning.
Baron and Morris picked up where Big Mike left off. Despite
their determination to excel in every endeavor, both men
were deeply loved and admired by their fellows. They were
generous to friend and foe: in their business and in the
community they devoted their exceptional energies to
projects and pursuits which produced great benefits for the
political, charitable and commercial societies of this land
they regarded with such proud interest.

A dozen families dominated the economic and social life
of the capital city, and the Goldwater family was pre-em-
inent in this tight-knit circle. Without Josephine's vivacious
and resourceful personality, things might have been much
different and Baron recognized this.

The store catered to the carriage trade and Josephine
dominated the fashionable set. Baron never made any effort
to determine which came first. He was proud of his wife
and grateful to her. The store was the center of luxury spending. Jo was the recognized leader of the luxury spenders.

There were many families with more money. If Baron had any ambition to amass a personal fortune, he was thwarted by his desire to indulge his wife and family.

In the Phoenix of his childhood, Barry recalls a complete lack of social separation based on economic conditions.

John Henry Lewis, a Negro boy who went on to become the world's light-heavy weight champion, although younger, was a close personal friend. The city didn't have its first segregated school until long after Barry was enrolled at Staunton. He says now, "I had to go to school in Virginia before I learned anything about segregation. I never heard a Jew called a kike or referred to in any derogatory way until I went East. But until I left Arizona in 1923, I literally was unaware of any kind of racial prejudice."

The Goldwater home was headquarters for a youthful gang consisting of Harry Rosenzweig and his brother Newt, who lived a block south on Central Avenue, the sons of a pioneer jewelry merchant; John Loper, son of a school administrator; Bob Creighton, son of Ned Creighton, long-time Republican National Committeeman from Arizona; Watson Defty, whose father had mining interests; Tim Firth, now a successful dentist; Frank Schwentker, whose father represented Pacific Mutual Life Insurance Company and who is now a college professor; Marcus Kelly, who became a doctor and is now dead; and Ray Johnson, the present vice president of New York Life.

Baron, who had a dislike for physical exercise of any kind, encouraged his sons' interest in athletics.

"We had what we called the North Central Athletic Club," Barry says. "Headquarters was the second floor gym on the top of our garage. Newt Rosenzweig was always the president and we played sandlot baseball and football, and during World War I we dug our trenches in a vacant lot on the corner of Central and Roosevelt."

This one time playground is now prime downtown property and the location of Arizona's pioneer radio station KOY.

As a result of Josephine's influence, Barry was an active member of Trinity Cathedral, serving as altar boy and acolyte.

"The church had more influence in our lives then," he says. "The only dances we could go to were in the parish hall on Friday nights and the Sunday School teacher was the basketball coach of our church team. I don't know how much he knew about the Bible, but he used to bring a basketball to Sunday School and we were in our seats on time. Any kid who missed was benched."

Dean William Scarlett, D.D., who went on to become Bishop of Missouri, was a particular favorite of the youngsters, and Barry speaks fondly of Billy Mitchell who was then Bishop of the Missionary District of Arizona.

"They both would disapprove of me now," he says. "Scarlett became quite a liberal, and I don't think Bishop Mitchell has much use for a conservative, but they were fine men and they made God a part of our everyday life when we were kids.

"It was a great privilege to read the lesson in church, and we listened to the sermons. They came to our basketball games and our picnics and never tut-tutted us when we got into trouble. I guess what I'm trying to say is, they weren't sanctimonious. They worshipped God in His church. They also gave us the notion that a friendly happy God could be with us on the basketball court or in school and when we got into kid's scrapes. Nobody scoffed at us for going to church. We loved God just as we loved our mother and father, and when Henry Miller brought a basketball to our Sunday School class, we kids didn't accept this as an invitation to goof off."

The North Central Athletic Club benefited materially from Baron's buying trips to New York. He came home with athletic apparatus, new games, and a variety of sports equipment. He encouraged his boys to compete and was particularly proud when Bob demonstrated a superior aptitude for golf.

Barry has an especially fond memory for Mabel Latham, a sixth grade teacher who was the daughter of Captain William Hancock, an early pioneer who surveyed the original Phoenix town site. The years have dimmed those sixth grade subjects, but Barry and his close friend Harry Rosenzweig remember that Mabel Latham made their sixth grade a memorable year.

"I don't remember anything she taught us," Barry says. "But my year with her stands out above all the other school days. I think it was the force of her personality, or perhaps I was more receptive in that year, but it was she who aroused my first interest in Phoenix history, and it was in the sixth grade that I began to get a larger view of education. I've always had a tremendous respect for dedicated school teachers because of Mabel Latham."

Barry's grammar school grades indicate he was not a particularly diligent student. His classmates remember him as friendly, full of enthusiasm and absorbed in interests they did not share.

Newt Rosenzweig remembers that Barry was always interested in radio.

"He'd leave a ball game any day to go and tinker with a crystal set. And when Earl Nielson would let him work on the transmitter of the broadcasting station which was the forerunner of KOY, Barry was in seventh heaven."

"Actually," Barry says, "the only regular job I had as a boy was helping Nielson in his store."

Barry claims he was the first disc jockey in Arizona.

"We'd turn on the power and I'd sit before the microphone and repeat the call letters, count from one to ten, and then play a phonograph record. Sometimes they'd hear us in Mesa, sixteen miles away."

Long after he was married, Mun told Barry that she and Baron had almost given up on their first-born because of his almost daily involvement in some sort of a fist fight. Barry doesn't recall the fights, but he does remember that John Henry Lewis' father, whom everybody called "Old Grey Dad" taught all the boys in Phoenix of that period how to box.

In the universal pattern of young boys feeling their oats, Phoenix youngsters gravitated to different gangs. Barry recalls that he was always afraid of the Goodson Gang.

Mel Goodson today is a sedate middle-aged business man, mild in manner and highly respected. Yet, according to Barry, he once led the toughest entourage in the southwest.

"I see old Mel today and he's such a mild-tempered, almost meek fellow, it's hard to make anyone believe that he was the roughest, toughest guy who ever hit this town. We called him 'Bull Goodson,' and when he came down the street we got on the other side. Henry Miller, the basketball coach at the church, finally ended the Goodson gang. He got Mel on our basketball team, and of course once we started playing together there wasn't much point in continuing the feuds."

Barry graduated from the eighth grade at Kenilworth, a

newly established grammar school on Fifth Avenue, a few blocks north of Roosevelt Street.

Barry's first year in high school was an amazingly successful period, in every aspect, outside the academic purpose. He was elected president of the freshman class, played freshman basketball and football, and for the first time in his life gave an indication of his potential for personal popularity which has contributed so greatly to his political career. When final grades were announced, Baron and Josephine learned their first-born son had flunked miserably. They decided it would take the discipline of a military school to make up for what they regarded as their indulgence.

The following year Barry entered Staunton Military Academy in Virginia. Four years later he graduated with full honors and received recognition for his outstanding service in the cadet corps, thus completely vindicating his parents' judgement.

The years at Staunton are full of contradictions. Barry was not a particularly good or diligent student. In academic matters, he just managed to get by. Military training appealed to him and he was an eager participant in the school's athletic program.

"Goldwater was one of the best cadets we ever turned out," says his military commander. "But there were times when we thought we would never get him through the school."

If the four years at Staunton did nothing else, they gave Barry an understanding which stretched far beyond the provincial limits of Arizona. He made friendships in school which still endure, and his interest in military affairs has affected his entire life. His most vivid memories are of the athletic activities and the commander's daughter.

In those days, the trip from Arizona to Virginia was accomplished by taking a train to Chicago, and then transfer-
ring to one of the lines leading south. One of Barry's return
trips, following a Christmas vacation spent in Arizona, coin-
cided with a necessary buying trip to New York for Baron.

Barry had arranged to meet some of his classmates in
Chicago and journey together on the second lap of the trip.
Baron decided to accompany his son.

In the confusion of the student reunion on the railroad car
after departing Chicago, there was no proper introduction
of the elder Goldwater.

"He might have been in the club car or the diner," Barry
says, "at any rate he wasn't around when we got together
and decided to play a little poker. After about thirty minutes,
I looked up and saw Dad standing in the aisle, and about this
time one of the players excused himself, leaving a vacant
place at the table."

Baron Goldwater, complete with wing collar, elegant
waistcoat and pince-nez glasses made his way to the table
and inquired if the boys would mind if he joined them. Ben
Harris, whose home was in Champaign, Illinois, and who
professed to a great degree of sophistication, surveyed the
elder Goldwater carefully and appeared considerably upset
when Barry invited his father to take the vacant seat. In a
moment or two, Ben excused himself and summoned Barry
to the other end of the car.

"Good Lord, Goldwater, don't you see what you've done?
We can't play poker with that fellow. He's one of those
travelling card sharks who ride the railroad trains."

When Barry stopped laughing, he said, "I really don't
think so, Ben. He's my father."

Barry, who had been forced to repeat his high school

freshman year at Staunton, graduated in 1928. The following fall he entered the University of Arizona at Tucson. His
plan was to take a liberal arts course with some special emphasis on business administration, a plan interrupted by the
death of his father.

"My idea was to have a good time in college and then
enter the family business. I had enough sense to know that
I wasn't a particularly apt student. I found it extremely
difficult to give my attention to a subject which didn't particularly appeal to me. It was good to be home and I meant
to make the most of it."

Barry, who frequently speaks disparagingly of his ability
as a student, overlooks or neglects to mention those areas
where he demonstrated outstanding ability. In his four years
at Staunton, he had completed all of the military requirements to qualify for an officer's commission, actually exceed-
ing ROTC college requirements.

It was inconvenient for the University of Arizona to recognize Goldwater's military status. Had this been done, he
would have outranked college seniors in the ROTC program.

The varsity football squad was short of centers and the
regular holder of that berth, Marvin Gentry, weighed only
155 pounds.

Barry was a fine football player, substituting as center at
first, though he was only a freshman.

Playing freshman basketball Barry suffered an aggravation
of his old knee injury, a disability which still causes him
great inconvenience at times. Once he gave up piloting an
airplane for five years because it was too difficult to squeeze
into a crowded cockpit. The basketball injury ended his
horseback riding, but he made Sigma Chi Fraternity, was
elected president of the freshman class and established him-

self firmly as a University of Arizona supporter, a position which in later years had a good deal to do with his election to the United States Senate.

CHAPTER **VII**

# THE RESTLESS YEARS

NINETEEN HUNDRED and twenty-nine marks the end
of the era many Americans old enough to remember would
like to forget. Between the end of World War I, officially
over on the eleventh of November, 1918, and the great stock
market crash, the life of the republic is characterized by a
flamboyant lawlessness usually attributed to the passage of
the Volstead Act. More than a single national law was involved. The western world was infected with an hysterical
desire to crowd out and overcome the agonizing memories
of broken promises, shattered illusions and the accusing,
questioning eyes of the dead and the dying.

In this period, bright young men dedicated their energies
to nonsense. It was fashionable to be skeptical. Old established values were no longer cherished. The ugly realities of
the greed and hate of the old world had cast their shadow
on the life of the new continent. Young America chose the

scoffer's seat. Money was meant to be spent. Nothing in life, least of all life itself, was sacred.

In this period, Barry Goldwater's failure to complete successfully the required courses in his freshman year in high school was something to laugh and joke about. Pleasure was all that really mattered. The hobnailed boots of the Kaiser's legions had destroyed all the beautiful and fair young men. Life itself was a ghastly joke and only the dull-witted clods still believed. It was the stock market that mattered; the market and the country club and the incredible speed of the Chrysler Seventy. Men boasted of the excellence of their bootleggers and jeered at the sacrifices of their fathers. The Russians wore hair on their faces and polished military boots; drank vodka and talked nonsense. In Germany, a madman named Hitler attracted a nondescript following to a beer bust in Munich. The government of France fell, was reformed, fell again.

In England and America men laid their lives on the altar of prosperity. Their gospel was the jargon of commerce; their epistles were letters of credit, and the young in every land, instinctively recognizing that life had lost its purpose, articulated their rebellion in vulgar hedonistic rituals.

A serious faced young man named Charles Lindbergh flew the Atlantic for a cash prize and the crowds went wild, never once recognizing that their hero had broken the chains of time and distance. Bootblacks had their favorite stockbrokers and stockbrokers had their favorite speakeasies. Machine guns spilled blood on the streets of Chicago and the sidewalks of Manhattan. Al Capone and Dutch Schultz and Detroit's Purple Gang became national heroes.

At the University of Arizona, Barry Goldwater played football and basketball, pledged Sigma Chi and found little in the classrooms of significant substance to challenge his interest.

In Phoenix the old order was changing. Farmers, who had made millions in cotton during the war and escaped the collapse of the cotton market with whole financial skins, were planting winter vegetables. Johnny-come-latelies were muscling out the old pioneer names. The money making fever produced land speculation and the dreamers predicted a great new future for Arizona as a winter resort.

The Goldwater store on North First Street was still fashion headquarters for the state, but the prosaic profits of merchandising were drab and uninteresting when compared to the commercial castles conjured up by the promoters and offered as the realities of tomorrow.

The McArthur brothers purchased thirteen hundred acres of desert land from some incredibly optimistic homesteaders who had laid claim to the cactus and mountains ten miles north of the city limits outside the irrigation district. Citizens with any sense knew very well the land was worthless. The homesteaders had settled on their selection in desperation because nothing else was left. Most of them sold out for a song and a promise—eager to be out from under their bad bargain. The price was good because it was more than they paid, and developing the land for a useful economic purpose was beyond their ability and completely out of range of their imagination or vision.

Baron Goldwater, a child of the frontier whose roots were deep in the uncompromising brutality of an untamed savage land, had lived most of his life as a citizen of two worlds. Like the linguist who translates an alien tongue into local idiom and familiar phrase, Big Mike's luxury-loving, fastidious, discriminating youngest boy had made a business of bringing the material elegance of the East within reach of his home town neighbors and customers.

The shelves of the Goldwater store were stocked with goods bearing commonplace descriptions—cottons and silks and leathers and furs—but the commodity really merchandised was class. For a lack of a more definite description, Baron's billheads bore the slogan, "The Best Always." More than half a century of living on the western frontier, while at the same time enjoying the sophisticated supply centers of New York, Chicago and San Francisco, gave Baron a perspective denied to many of his fellow residents. Baron's business judgment, supported by his knowledge of that portion of America centered on the East bank of the Hudson River, quickly recognized the merchandising value of Arizona's matchless sunshine and mild winters. When the McArthur brothers came to him with their projected winter resort hotel, he opened his check book and climbed aboard their bandwagon.

During all the years of their married life, Josephine and Baron enjoyed a true partnership. Baron had been aloof and shy in his relationship with the children, but this was not from choice. He had found it impossible to meet his youngsters on the same common ground they enjoyed with Josephine. But there had been no secrets between husband and wife until one day in the early twenties when Baron's family physician diagnosed his patient's newly found symptoms as a heart disease, angina pectoris. Big Mike's son had no intention of abandoning his customary habits or becoming a semi-invalid. He intended to enjoy whatever was left of life, free from the crippling inhibitions which are invariably imposed when such knowledge is shared with family and friends. Baron thanked his doctor, put on his shirt, coat and necktie, adjusted his pince-nez and extracted a promise that the doctor's findings should remain a secret between them.

The night the McArthur brothers' dream hostelry on the edge of the desert opened for guests marked the beginning of Phoenix as a resort area. The Arizona Biltmore Hotel, designed by Albert Chase McArthur, a student and follower of Frank Lloyd Wright, ushered in a plush magnificence never before available between Chicago and San Francisco. Its exterior of concrete was simple and functional; its interior haughty and grand and unmistakably expensive.

Baron Goldwater was there with a crew of models and decorators and window dressers to put on a style show. It was necessary to impress the overflow crowd of Easterners with the Goldwater name, and the models paraded in revealing fabrics under the banner of impressive American and European labels.

All of Arizona that counted, that is anyone who had money or credit, was in the audience that night. The opening was a smashing success and when Baron climbed the stairs to his bedroom in the big house on North Central Avenue he was satisfied. The hotel was bound to succeed. More important, the occupants of those $50 a day rooms at the Arizona Biltmore would make their Arizona purchases at Goldwater's.

Josephine had not gone to the opening. It was a store-sponsored show and the store was Baron's domain; in addition, she was scheduled to play her second round match in the country club's women's tournament, and Josephine took her golf seriously.

At 8:15 the following morning, March 6, 1929, Mrs. Baron Goldwater was on the first tee. At the end of her eighth hole, she was two up and victory appeared certain. Suddenly, without offering any explanation, she told her caddy to put the clubs back in the locker room, forfeited the match to a surprised opponent and walked hurriedly to her car in the parking lot. Later, she told her children:

"I knew something was wrong. I don't know how I knew it—I didn't know what it was, but suddenly I just couldn't finish the match. I had to get home."

Her husband was still in bed when Josephine knocked and entered his room shortly after ten o'clock on that morning. His presence home at that hour and the lines of pain on his face were enough to send Jo racing to the telephone, in disobedience of Baron's protest.

When she came back to the bedroom, she took her husband's hand and urged him not to try to talk.

"The doctor's on his way. Everything will be all right."

Baron nodded. He had known this pain before but never of such intensity. He was sixty-three years old and life had been incredibly good to him. His affairs were in order, and his store was prosperous, and now that Josephine was beside him he had no complaints.

The pain grew worse. He smiled, attempted to say something, and then as though he realized there was nothing which needed to be said, he relaxed on the comfortable bed in the room which had been his for so many years.

When the doctor, whose office was only seven blocks down the street, arrived, Baron Goldwater was dead.

Josephine had embraced all the gay moments of life with an almost reckless enthusiasm. Now she accepted her burden of grief with courage. Her life was over but there were still years to be lived. She made the necessary arrangements, summoned her children home from school, and when Baron's casket was lowered into its grave, she turned her face forward to the years ahead.

The family now says Barry left school immediately following his father's death to come home and shoulder a portion of responsibility in the store. This is probably more fiction than fact. The store was under the capable management of Sam Wilson, who had been with the organization since 1909. Sam was far more qualified to steer the store through the difficult days of the depression than ex-college freshman, Barry.

Big Mike had insisted his sons serve their apprenticeships. Baron had worked as a salesman in San Francisco, and as a junior clerk in the Prescott store before he was admitted to full partnership with his brothers. Barry went to work in the Phoenix store as a junior clerk. The fact that his name was Goldwater bought no special preferences.

"It didn't take me long to find out who I was or what was expected of me," Barry says now. "Sam let me know I was on trial and Mun backed him up. I sold everything in the store with the exception of brassieres and corsets. I swept out, counted stock, measured yard goods, made deliveries and earned twenty dollars a week."

Sam Wilson was a stern taskmaster. A bachelor, he had enjoyed an extremely close relationship with Baron and Josephine. He regarded Barry, Bob and Carolyn with the same affection a man might have for his own children. But he tolerated no nonsense in the store. During working hours Barry was just another apprentice clerk who must prove his ability if he wanted to advance.

After the 1952 Senatorial campaign, Ernest McFarland, the Democratic incumbent Barry defeated, sneeringly referred to his victorious Republican opponent as a "ribbon clerk." When some tale-bearer reported this, hoping to incite a display of temper, Barry only smiled and said:

"That's right, I was a ribbon clerk. I was a shoe clerk. I sold calico and greeting cards and dishes, but you tell Mr. McFarland that I was a damn good ribbon clerk. The second year I was in the store, I set an all-time record for individual sales, and I have a great admiration and fondness for people who work in retail establishments. If that's what Mac wants to call me, tell him I'm proud to be a ribbon clerk. The people I know who work at this trade are honest and enterprising and determined to give their customers value received for every dollar spent. Tell Mr. McFarland that's the way I intend to conduct myself when I'm sitting in his old seat in the Senate."

Barry still regards himself as a salesman, and it was his campaigns to sell the people of Arizona on the potential development of the Colorado River and Arizona's future as a tourist center which ultimately led to his decision to enter politics.

In those early years of the depression, apprentice-clerk Goldwater learned all the problems of a retail merchant firsthand from bitter experience. While other luxury establishments were closing their doors, Goldwater's stayed open and struggled to keep the customers coming in.

Bob was at the University of Illinois and later on at Stanford University. Carolyn was at school and Barry lived with Mun in the North Central House. For almost the first time in his life he found all of his talents challenged. He worked hard, asked for no special privileges and received none. He also played hard. The world of commerce might be on its deathbed, but Baron's oldest son was twenty-one and he had no intention of going into a decline just because the nation's economy was all out of kilter. He managed to finance his activities on the $20 a week he drew at the store.

Nogales, Arizona, is directly across the international border from Nogales, Sonora, in Mexico. The Mexican city offered a gaiety and frivolity not available in prohibition America. The Cave, a *turista* restaurant, housed in an old jail, rough and unfinished, was a favorite gathering spot for excitement hungry *Americanos*. The bull fights, the Latin holiday spirit and the free flowing *cerveza* attracted a substantial number of Arizonans of all ages on weekends.

One Saturday night after the store closed, Barry, A. J. Bayless and Paul Morris decided they needed a night on the town in Nogales, Sonora. The border is almost two hundred miles from Phoenix, and by the time the trio reached its destination it was daylight. They decided to have breakfast at one of the numerous sidewalk cafes.

A. J. Bayless, now a middle-aged respected grocery merchant who operates the most outstanding chain of supermarkets in Arizona today, broke into a series of belly laughs when he was asked to verify the unusual activities of this particular trip.

Somewhere the revelers found a violinist, a bull fiddler and a trumpeter to serenade them. After driving most of the night, the Mexican beer was especially welcome. Just as Barry was beginning to enjoy his *chile con huevos*, Paul Morris decided Goldwater would look good with a face full of beer. The brew was cold and pungent, it dripped on the eggs in a particularly doleful and disappointing way. Barry responded with the handiest thing he could find—a jar of mustard. But the dripping beer spoiled his aim and the glass jar with its sticky, yellow condiment sailed past the chest of Barry's tormentor.

The laughter of the three gay blades was suddenly drowned in an outburst of uncomplimentary Spanish adjectives. Goldwater wiped the beer from his eyes, looked past his partners in fun to discover the mustard jar had shattered on the shiny badge of an extremely tall and now extremely angry member of the Nogales *policía*.

The mustard had splattered like a starburst across the khaki uniform shirt and, until this instant, spotless polished Sam Browne belt.

Official dignity would not be swayed or soothed. The *Americanos* were herded into their own car for the trip to the *estación policía* with the mustard-smeared servant of the law very much in command in the back seat.

Barry had twenty-three dollars in his billfold—one week's wages plus three more lonely bills he'd saved from his prior pay envelope. Knowing the appetite of Mexican officialdom for gringo money, Goldwater wisely but cautiously slipped the billfold out of his hip pocket and thrust it down between the seat cushions.

Bayless was driving. Goldwater, suffering from a flare-up of his basketball knee, was stiffly erect in the right hand front seat. Paul and the outraged mustard-smeared public official were in the back. When they arrived at the police station, less than a block from the international border, Goldwater descended slowly to the ground. A. J. and Paul jumped from the car and raced to the border. This sudden action caught their captor completely off guard. Barry, a little unsteady on his shaky knee, blocked the policeman's path long enough for his fleeing companions to reach the border and freedom.

The baffled Mexican pointed his drawn pistol at Goldwater and motioned towards the plain adobe building with its grim steel-barred windows.

Inside a mustached member of *la guardia* relieved Barry of his personal possessions, led him to a room at the end of the hall and slammed the steel latticed door in his face. The red-eyed sun leered over the tops of the Duquesne Mountains to the East and stared in through the open window. Somewhere a trumpeter rehearsed the arresting melodic prelude to a bullfight. Goldwater sat on the edge of his iron bunk and confidently expected to be rescued.

Before an hour had passed, he heard an American voice at the end of the hallway demanding to know if *el carcelero* had in his custody one American named Barry Goldwater.

The American voice was familiar, and when the approaching footsteps ended in the hallway before the door, Goldwater recognized the son of a prominent Nogales, Arizona, family who had lived in the Sigma Chi house when Barry was at the University in Tucson.

The American peered in at the prisoner and after a long moment turned away. "Éste hombre no es Goldwater."

The first time it was funny and even Barry could see the humor of it, but when two more alleged rescuers had come down the hall, stared at him without any sign of recognition, and then turned away in denial, the joke began to lose its flavor.

Barry banged on the door and demanded *el jefe de policía*. Finally the chief, a handsome and erect official, was summoned.

"You will be quiet, *señor,* or your punishment will be doubled," he said in faultless English with only a whisper of an accent.

"But I have to get out of here," Goldwater protested.

"The fine is fixed at fifty dollars in the money of *Estados Unidos del Norte*. The property clerk tells me you have no money."

"Can I write a check?" Barry asked.

The check, perhaps, if the chief could be assured the check would be paid. This prisoner had claimed to be Goldwater, but the Americanos who had come to see him said no, he was not by that name.

Barry, with just the proper amount of hesitancy, admitted he had attempted to deceive his captors. Goldwater was not his name. He was the son of a very prominent Phoenix grocer, J. B. Bayless. If the chief had been in Phoenix perhaps he was acquainted with the Bayless stores?

The chief had been in Phoenix, in fact he had been in the Bayless stores and he would be delighted to accept such a check. The blanks were secured, the check was drawn, and with a flourish Barry signed the name "A. J. Bayless."

"There was nothing else I could do," Barry argues. "Everyone who had come to see me said I wasn't Goldwater. I had to be somebody and I knew how to spell Bayless."

*El jefe* dropped his stern manner, ordered the prisoner and the prisoner's car released.

When the check was presented at the Phoenix bank, an alert clerk questioned the signature and called A. J. before approving payment.

"At first I said hell, no, I didn't write any checks in Mexico," A. J. remembers. "Then I got to thinking. Goldwater had seemed pretty self-satisfied when he came across that border. He said they never would have let him out if he hadn't mentioned my name, and he told Paul to remember that anytime he got in trouble in Nogales, Sonora, just to call the chief of police and mention the name A. J. Bayless. I told the bank to pay the check. I wish I had it now. It would be quite a souvenir."

It was during this period in his life that Barry learned to fly. He took his first lessons from an instructor named Jack Thornberg who was operating from a dirt strip on West Christy Road. When Barry got ready to solo, operations had been moved to a new location on the East side of town, and Barry's first solitary flight was from the forerunner of what is now Phoenix Sky Harbor, a fine metropolitan airport.

The Great Lakes biplane owned by Thornberg was an exceptionally fine aircraft for its time, and the inverted four cylinder engine made it ideal for aerobatics. Barry, who has flown almost every type of airplane from that day to this and is one of two members of the Senate qualified in the one hundred series fighter jets, still admits a fondness for that stubby-winged aircraft in which he made his maiden flight.

In the Senator's Washington office, he has a collection of models of all the aircraft he has piloted. The little Great Lakes biplane enjoys a prominent position in that array of more than seventy airplanes which span a period of more than thirty years.

Flying is still very much a part of the Senator's life. He relaxes when in the air. A cautious pilot, he maintains his sharp instrument proficiency by regular periods of training in ground simulators. Goldwater's only accident occurred as a result of an abortive take-off attempt crosswind in a rudderless Air Coupe, which leaves the pilot helpless in a surface wind from the side. The accident occurred on a dirt strip in the Navajo section of Arizona. It was necessary to disassemble the airplane for transportation to Phoenix by truck.

The driver pulled into a station at Wickenburg and tore the airplane all to pieces on the station canopy. "It would have been a cinch to fix what I did to it," Barry says, "but that Standard Oil steel roof was too much. We junked it."

Despite the fact that he learned to fly in a minimum amount of time, and has long been recognized by his professional contemporaries as a sharp pilot, Barry still suffers from a sense of guilt over those student days.

"Turbulence builds up rapidly when sun-induced thermal activity begins to take place," Goldwater explains. "My early lessons all began at six o'clock in the morning. I would sneak out of the house, go to the airport, fly for an hour and be in the store long before it opened. But I didn't tell Mun what I was doing. It's the only secret I ever tried to keep from her."

Barry's mother was not deceived.

"I knew he was up to something. I just hoped it wasn't something really bad, but since he didn't tell me, I didn't ask him."

She learned the secret of Barry's early morning departures when a piece in the local newspaper announced that Barry Goldwater had acquired a private pilot's license.

"When he came home," Mun says, "I asked him if he thought I was too old to share his ambitions."

Barry never again kept anything from his mother. When Bob graduated from college and indicated a desire to follow Barry's example, Mun encouraged her second son.

In Arizona, the economic cycle hit bottom in 1932. No one has ever satisfactorily explained why it took the great depression three years to spread its paralyzing fingers across the western half of the nation. Perhaps the West was just slower to comprehend the significance of the stock market break.

Sam Wilson had wisely anticipated the declining sales. The store still featured the same quality and some of the expensive merchandise, but there was less of it on the shelves and other more popular-priced items were added.

Recalling this period, Barry says, "It was touch and go for awhile. We had to reduce salaries and there were several times we were not sure we could make the payroll, but no employee was discharged and we never filed a lawsuit to collect an overdue account."

Even in those depression years, there were a fortunate few who had ready cash available. These were the people who had been long-time customers of the store. The luxury buying habits of Arizona were firmly established—a special dress for graduation had to come from Goldwater's—no society bride would accept a substitute for the Goldwater label. Dozens of luxuries were sacrificed to grim reality, but Goldwater's refused to compromise on quality.

"My dad had just one fixed notion about the business," Barry says. "He insisted that our store have the best always. Sam Wilson and I were determined to keep it that way."

In the years since that trying period, the store has expanded, moved, expanded again and established additional outlets. The reputation of having the best always is as bright as it was when Baron suggested to Josephine that her trousseau should come from the best store in the territory.

Despite this reputation for being an exclusive store, Goldwater's was never snooty or "uptown." No prospective customer was ever made to feel uncomfortable in that manner practiced by expensive New York shops.

"We really never made a great profit on the high-priced things," Barry says. "The customers who built the store were the office girls and stenographers who wanted to keep up their appearance and recognized the value of quality." He insists Goldwater prices are not any higher than comparable quality at competitive stores.

During his apprenticeship, while Sam Wilson was still in actual command of the operation, Barry earned a reputation among other merchants of being a "loner." "He wanted to run the store according to his own ideas," says a competitor, "and while he might cooperate on any project which promised benefit for the downtown area, he just wasn't about to accept the group's thinking in regard to closing hours and holidays. He wasn't a rebel exactly, but he was mighty independent. At the same time, he made a number of suggestions which benefited all of us."

When Bob Goldwater graduated from Stanford and returned to Phoenix, Sam Wilson had left the store and Barry was in complete charge. The brothers decided it would be wise for Bob to commence his business career in the employ of the Valley National Bank.

"You learn about managing money," Barry said, "and I'll keep on at the sales end. Then after a few years, we'll combine what we've learned and do what no Goldwater has ever been able to do—we'll make a fortune."

They might have done it, too, if a madman named Hitler had not been intent on conquering the world—if the concept of a big brother paternalistic central state had not intrigued Franklin D. Roosevelt—if Karl Marx and Friedrich Engles had never combined to publish a dull and tedious treatise on dialectical materialism.

# CHAPTER VIII

## FORSAKING ALL OTHERS

MARGARET JOHNSON was a student at the exclusive Mt. Vernon Seminary in Washington, D. C. when she first met Barry Goldwater. Her parents, the senior Ray Prescott Johnsons of Muncie, Indiana, were spending the winter in Phoenix hoping the mild climate would benefit Peggy's older brother who was suffering from bronchial complications. The introduction took place in the Goldwater store in December, 1930.

Margaret was twenty years old, a petite brown-haired girl with deep blue eyes and a beautiful complexion. She had been in Arizona less than a week and hated it.

"I remember thinking Barry was extremely handsome and very well-dressed. He had on a pleated shirt and a rather severe necktie. He reminded me of the boys I'd known in the East and I was miserably homesick."

Almost thirty years earlier, Josephine Williams, who had

come West because of a health problem, went into the Goldwater store to make a modest purchase and ultimately married the bachelor who owned the store. Ann Johnson wanted
her daughter to meet Barry Goldwater. She had no thought
of romance, but Barry was a leader in the younger social
set and Ann wanted Margaret to make friends and have fun
during her holiday visit.

The Ray Prescott Johnsons had taken a lease on the
country club residence belonging to United States Senator
Carl Hayden. Although Hayden had been in Congress since
statehood, he maintained a home in Phoenix which he rented
during the winter season when the Senate was in session.

For more than fifty years the Johnson family had been
prominent in the business and social life of Muncie. Margaret's father was president of the Warner Gear Company.
In 1928 Warner Gear, Marvel Carburetor and the Borg and
Beck Clutch Company were merged and Borg-Warner was
born. Margaret's father served as Executive Vice President
of Borg-Warner until his death.

Christmas in Muncie would have been a happy time, a
renewal of old friendships and a round of holiday parties.
To be away from home at Christmas time was a small price
to pay for their son's health, but Margaret's parents realized
it would be a difficult two weeks for their daughter. Ann
determined to do what she could to mitigate Peggy's natural
disappointment at not being home.

Girls have always been susceptible to the charm of Baron
Goldwater's older son.* His critics today ruefully admit that
Barry gets the women's votes because he radiates virility, but

---

* When Barry read this page of the manuscript, he noted in red pencil,
"Very doubtful from experience."

the homesick girl from Muncie says now she was not particularly impressed.

Barry remembers thinking Peggy was quite attractive, but extremely shy and reserved. They had no dates, and although Peggy came to one Christmas party at the house on North Central Avenue, it wasn't Barry who invited her.

"I'd gone over to the country club with Mother and Daddy," Peggy says. "Everyone there was over fifty with the exception of Herb Green, who was there with his mother. Herb and I tried to dance but the music was about thirty years beyond us. He asked me if I wanted to go to Barry's house.

"What I really wanted to do was go back to Muncie, to do the things I'd always done at holiday times, but I thought anything would be better than that country club. (When you're twenty, anyone fifty is ancient). I said I'd be glad to go.

"Herb took me to Barry's. The basement was decorated and so full of young people you could hardly see the decorations. They had an orchestra and everybody was having a great time. Later on Bob did some impersonations and I remember it was a pleasant party, but there was nothing very special about this one and Barry didn't make any fuss over me. I'd heard so much about the Goldwaters, I was a little disappointed in that party."

Peggy doesn't know what she really expected. She says, "I guess I wanted them to live up to their reputation." Bob and Carolyn and Barry did have a reputation for doing wacky, uninhibited things. Friends recall the time when Bob and Barry decided they needed a little target practice with their twenty-twos and persuaded Carolyn to throw old phonograph records up in the air as substitute clay pigeons.

"We were pretty good shots," Barry admits with a grin, "but Mun didn't exactly approve of us using the basement as a shooting gallery."

The passing years have not lessened the Goldwaters' zest for life. On Barry's fiftieth birthday his brother Bob gave him a 1919 model fire engine—bright red and in complete working order with siren, bell, pressure tank and hose. Bob found it broken down and abandoned in a storage garage in a little Arizona town. With the aid of his son and their friends, the fire engine was completely refurbished for Uncle Barry.

"I couldn't think of anything to give him he didn't already have," Bob says, "and he was always crazy about going to fires."

Some of the neighbors on North Central Avenue recall the improvised cannon which the Goldwater youngsters fired on holidays. One time they actually loaded the old field piece with pieces of chain and old iron, trained it on a billboard across Central Avenue and scored a bull's-eye.

There was one birthday party when Peggy and Barry were living in their new home in Country Club Manor. Carolyn, who was then married to Paul Sexson, brought her brother a real live two-hundred pound pig with appropriate birthday greetings lettered on the pig's back. Everything went well until the frightened porker broke from his pen and wound up in the Goldwater swimming pool. Barry dove in with all his clothes on to retrieve the struggling animal. The birthday greetings which had been lettered with vegetable dye, dissolved in the water.

"Spoiled the best shirt I ever owned," Barry complains, "and if you think it's easy to get a two hundred pound pig out of a swimming pool you ought to try it sometime."

Following this episode, Barry found a piece of costume jewelry in the form of a pig pinned to his Red Cross life saving badge.

Margaret Johnson returned to the East, completed her school year at Mt. Vernon, and made plans to study at the Grand Central Art School in New York City. She was a serious student with a particular interest in fabrics and designing, and this led ultimately to a job with the David Crystal organization.

"I'd gone to school early one morning in 1932," Margaret says. "The instructor asked me if I knew anyone who might be interested in a job sketching for the Crystal people. I said, 'Why don't you let me apply?' He was somewhat shocked and I think embarrassed to tell me he lacked confidence in my ability."

Whatever the instructor's feelings might have been, the David Crystal organization hired Margaret at the end of that original interview. Before the end of the year her employers offered to promote her to designer.

In the apparel business, the manufacturer risks his entire success on the cleverness of the designer, and Margaret must have had a real flare to earn the confidence of this outstanding quality house. Margaret returned to her apartment that night filled with excitement and anticipation. For a girl barely in her twenties, such an offer was heady wine.

Her dream castles tumbled with a crash—she found a telegram informing her that her father had suffered a stroke in Phoenix.

Margaret left New York on the train that night. Her boss at David Crystal offered to hold the job open two weeks; beyond that he couldn't wait. Between trains in Chicago she talked with her mother by telephone and learned her father was making satisfactory progress.

Peggy didn't like Phoenix any better on her second visit in 1932 than on her first. During the anxious weeks of waiting, she encountered Barry casually at the club, in the store, but never in the evening. She and her father had been extremely close all of her life and she had no interest beyond his recovery.

In early November, 1932, with her father apparently out of immediate danger, it was decided that Margaret would return to New York, close her apartment, and rejoin the family in Phoenix.

Ray Prescott Johnson, Sr. died the night Margaret reached New York.

"Barry never knew Daddy," Margaret says. "I've always been sorry about that. They would have been great friends."

The finality of death was difficult for her to accept.

Margaret met her mother in Muncie, found comfort in the words of the minister as he quoted that great enduring Epistle of St. Paul's, and in her grief discovered new dignity and maturity.

That summer of 1933, spent at the Johnson's place in Charlevoix, Michigan, was a period of indecision. The job at David Crystal had been filled, but Margaret knew if she returned to New York, her talents would soon be put to use. The future was dim and blurred. It was comfortable just to relax and she put off making a decision.

Ann Johnson, despite her grief, refused to permit her children to withdraw from their activities because of their father's death. She encouraged the normal summertime activities. When some of Margaret's old beaus turned up she made them welcome.

Both Ann and her daughter were somewhat surprised when Barry Goldwater telephoned one morning from downtown Charlevoix to pay his respects and discover Peggy's plans for the evening.

Barry, who had come to stay one weekend, found excuses to extend his visit to two full weeks.

"He proposed the night he was to leave," Peggy says. "He was gay and tender and lots of fun. I wasn't ready for marriage; I told him so."

When summer was over, Margaret decided against returning to New York and instead went back with her mother and brother to the family home in Muncie. A life of ease and luxury was open to her, but the social world did not appeal to Margaret. She opened a dress shop of her own which did surprisingly well commercially. Ann Johnson approved. She had encouraged her daughter's ambition to put her artistic talent to work in New York. The Johnsons were doers. From a financial standpoint there was no necessity for Peggy to work. But unproductive idleness was incompatible with family tradition. Peggy's dress shop was not a plaything subsidized by the family fortune. It made money because its owner had talent and determination.

Barry continued his courtship by correspondence and long distance telephone. He sent nonsensical presents, cherished because they communicated Barry's unlimited zest for life. Margaret recognized that deep within this handsome, curly-haired young man there was an elfin spirit upstaging the gloomy realities and disappointments of the world. An impish, impulsive, tender spirit capable of great gaiety and depth, moving resolutely to meet whatever fortune had in store for him with a thumb placed to his nose for all the

petty meanness and narrow criticisms of the selfish, small
personalities barking at his heels.

Peggy remembers being at an airport somewhere in the
Middle West. After a rather abrupt parting from Barry, she
responded to a page on the loudspeaker system and a solemn
middle-aged delivery boy presented her with a caged love-
bird. "I gave the bird to a little boy who was getting off the
airplane," she says. "Barry had missed seeing me off when I
left Phoenix and this was his way of saying he was sorry."

On another occasion, Peggy was travelling between Chicago and Phoenix on the Southern Pacific. The porter delivered a box of apples to her roomette. When she arrived in
Phoenix, she learned the train was full of doctors headed
West for a medical convention.

"No one else will ever understand what this has meant to
me," she says. "I've never had a dull moment or any kind
of unhappiness which he caused. I think I'm one of the
luckiest girls in the world."

There were tears of joy in her eyes when she said this to
me on July 27, 1961, almost thirty years after that New
Year's Eve in Muncie.

Barry had come to Indiana at Christmas time. "He said
he was coming for the holidays," Peggy says, "but I didn't
believe him because I know how important the Christmas
season is in the store. But he turned up and we had a wonderful time together."

When the horns and a cannon boomed to celebrate the
advent of 1934, Barry took Peggy from the dance floor to a
phone booth.

"We're going to call your mother and wish her a happy
New Year," he said. When the greetings and wishes were
exchanged, Barry closed the phone booth door and proposed.

Peggy smiles about it now. "There wasn't any escape," she says. "I said yes, and we called Mother right back to tell her."

Margaret and her mother had planned to sail from New York on the ninth of January for a trip around the world. In the more sedate morning hours following his acceptance, Barry agreed the trip should be made on schedule. When his promised bride and her mother sailed from New York Harbor, Barry was on hand to bid them *bon voyage*.

The cruise took the Johnsons through the Panama Canal to a scheduled stop in Los Angeles. While the other passengers were occupied with the sights of Hollywood, Peggy and her mother were busy with an announcement dinner. Jo Goldwater and Carolyn came to the California city with Barry. If Peggy's friends were a little surprised, so were Barry's.

"I was afraid she might back out," Barry says now. "The dinner made it semi-official but I kept thinking about that six months cruise and the people she would meet on the boat and the fact that we would be separated all that time."

Barry, who insists his outlook is a practical one, totally devoid of sentiment, would probably accuse his wife of great exaggeration if he heard her account of the long distance courtship which followed.

"When we docked at the Hawaiian Islands, I found a whole packet of letters waiting for me," she says. "There were no dates on them, but on the envelopes I found explicit instructions. For example, one would say 'to be opened before breakfast on the first day at sea out of Hawaii.' Another, 'please read this before your first drink in the evening.' There was a special group to be read at midnight on moonlight nights—one or more letters for every day she was at sea.

"It was the same when we docked at Tahiti, Australia, and Ceylon."

Peggy still has the letters.

"When Barry was overseas in World War II," Peggy says, "the children got the same kind of warm, loving, expressive communications. Letters and presents; hilarious and ridiculous presents; impractical useless, inexpensive expressions of a father's love for his children."

Peggy and Barry were married in Grace Episcopal Church in Muncie, Indiana, on September 22, 1934. "I took instructions from Bishop William D. Scarlett and was confirmed in the Episcopal Church shortly before we were married," Peggy says. "Dad had been a Baptist; Mother was an Episcopalian when she married him, but she always went to Dad's church. I wanted to be a part of Barry's life."

This act of unity is symbolic of their marriage.

"Barry loved the Indian reservations," Peggy says, "so I went with him to the reservations." On one occasion in 1937 they travelled twelve hundred miles through Navajo land in a jeep without going a single mile on an established road. It is difficult today to imagine the beautifully groomed Mrs. Barry Goldwater, coming from Mt. Vernon School, child of Muncie society, riding in a jeep, much less travelling this distance.

Exploring, hunting, fishing, searching for Indian ruins, poking into out-of-the-way places, all these things Peggy has done with great enthusiasm. She has washed prints in the dark room for her husband's photographic work, cooked over a camp fire, slept on the ground in a bed roll, embracing all of her husband's hobbies with one exception—she has an abnormal fear of flying and is never comfortable in an airplane.

"I fly with Barry now," she says, "but I'm still frightened. Though I would rather be scared with Barry than in a hotel room or an apartment or at home without him."

The newly-married couple returned to an apartment at 18 East Garfield Street in Phoenix and Peggy found herself involved in a host of civic responsibilities. She was active in the Junior League and as Barry's wife there were constant demands to accept membership on boards of various civic and charitable organizations.

The apartment was much too small.

"We had a darkroom in the kitchen and half the time I couldn't do the dinner dishes because Barry was developing pictures. Then he would want to go on a trip and we would have to search for a week for all the equipment which had been parcelled out for storage between the store and Mun's and anybody who had extra space in their garage."

The pressure was too much and they rented a home in the Encanto District. They were living there when their first child, Joanne, was born on January 18, 1936.

"I wanted a boy," Peggy says, "Barry wanted a girl. This time he had his way."

The score is even now—Barry, Jr., born July 15, 1938, and Mike on March 15, 1940, named for his grandfather, and Peggy, Jr., on July 27, 1944.

Joanne's name was a combination of Barry's mother's name and Peggy's mother's name.

Three weeks after Joanne was born, Barry and Peggy moved into a new home in a new subdivision, then considered to be on the outskirts of Phoenix. A developer had purchased acreage west of the Phoenix Country Club, north of Thomas Road. When the venture failed to capture public support, the Valley National Bank which financed the project urged its loyal customers to consider the area.

This was in 1936 and the development called Country Club Manor was outside the city limits. Today the Phoenix city boundaries are more than twenty miles to the north and the Country Club is surrounded by business and residential development.

The new house was a great adventure, unconventional in design, featuring a lavish use of glass brick—something new in building then—with a rumpus and dark room occupying the entire basement.

"Life was so simple," Peggy says, speaking nostalgically of those years now. "I wanted Barry to be the greatest merchant in the world and I think he might very well have been. He wanted to explore Arizona, take pictures, involve his children in his own enthusiasms. Aside from the buying trips to New York, we were pretty much like any other young established couple with children and responsibilities."

There were problems and moments of gaiety. Both Carolyn and Bob were married—Bob to a girl whose family name was Johnston and Carolyn to her childhood sweetheart, Paul Sexson. Mun was suffering from an undiagnosed illness which eventually sent her to Mayo's in Rochester for surgery in the spring of 1936.

Summers for the most part were spent in Phoenix. The Goldwaters had a cabin in the mountains at Groom Creek south of Prescott. The year his first-born son was three, Barry took over an entire hotel at the Hassayampa Mountain Club and used it for a vacation spot, not only for his family but the store's long-time employees. The acquisition of the hotel for the summer paralleled Big Mike's operation of the stamp mill on the Hassayampa so long ago.

At the Chicago Convention on July 27, 1960, when Margaret Goldwater heard Paul Fannin, the Governor of Arizona, nominate her husband for President of the United States, there were tears in her eyes—tears of pride and joy and also tears of apprehension.

"These years of Barry's being in politics have separated the family," she says. "I know he's doing what he must do, but at times I'm frightened. Not long ago I read in a national magazine that President Kennedy doesn't joke any more, doesn't have time for laughter, doesn't have time for his friends, and it frightens me to think this might happen to Barry. It's bad enough now." And she smiles and quotes one of her husband's oft-repeated statements: " 'We have to pay rent for the space we occupy.' And I guess he's right. Barry won't let the rent go unpaid."

CHAPTER IX

## BEFORE PEARL HARBOR

IN 1940 a cruel insanity possessed the minds of half the world, numbed the senses of reasonable men, and engulfed all human life in the senseless, merciless ambitions of Hitler and Mussolini.

The man with the umbrella made his pilgrimage to Munich and then practiced pious self-deception. Others in equally high positions closed their eyes and pretended the evil didn't exist because they could not see it. In Russia, Joseph Stalin played his waiting game with shrewd animal cunning, matching one side against the other, exploiting the hope of decent people while he catered and pandered to the egomaniac with the brown shirt and toothbrush mustache.

In America it was election time and Franklin Roosevelt, campaigning for his third term, was saying, "I've told you again, and again, and again. The United States will not enter this war." And the people believed because they wanted to believe, because the illusion was comforting and the reality too stark and ugly to behold.

In Arizona, thirty-one-year-old Barry Goldwater, father of two young children, young husband, civic leader, mainstay of a half-dozen charitable causes, had been "paying rent" by serving as chairman of the Community Chest drives, Vice President of the Chamber of Commerce, member of the board of St. Luke's Hospital, fund raiser for hospitals and active churchman.

During much of 1939 and 1940 he'd been on the road, travelling Arizona, speaking to service clubs, PTA's and business men on the Colorado River problem, documenting his talks with moving pictures he had taken from the air and on the ground.

"I argued with Bob that it was good public relations for the store," he explains, "but I was never able to prove it."

The store was doing as well as could be expected in a nation which had never fully recovered from the effects of the great depression. From display windows to the notions counters, Barry had systematically remodeled and refurnished; the resultant face lifting was an entirely new look. Not all the space was given over to merchandise. Stairways were lined with photographs of the early days, and Barry's own studies of Arizona Indians, printed with loving care in sepia tones at night in the Manor Drive darkroom, decorated the elevator walls and many of the display areas leading into departments.

Bob had left the bank and come into the store. The problems of management had lost the urgent challenge which had so completely absorbed all of Barry's energies during the decade which was closing.

Despite the incumbent President's soothing campaign

statements, the nation was beginning to build its military muscle, and Lt. Colonel Ennis C. Whitehead arrived in Phoenix to guide the development of a new military flying school on the desert thirty miles west of the city.

Arizona's turbulent skies give pilots a rough ride in summer time, but the magnificent visibility, the almost total lack of those circumstances which require instrument flying, make this area a natural Air Force choice for the training of young pilots. Buildings and runways and mechanical facilities were completed almost simultaneously with the arrival of the first contingent of confident, eager, prospective airmen. The President said there would be no war, but the cadets knew better. Each hour of off-duty time was precious and they meant to cram it with as much gaiety as their strong and capable hands could grasp.

The community responded with what was the forerunner of the world-wide USO organization. At first it was a haphazard, disorganized effort with various civic minded citizens seeking to seize the ball and drop it through their own particular personal hoop. There were dances at the country clubs and lawn parties and trips to the chain of man-made lakes on the Salt River. Second Lieutenant, Reserve Infantry Officer Barry Goldwater visited the new Luke Air Force Base with a contingent from the Chamber of Commerce.

"That place was unorganized chaos," he says now, "with no personnel, no operational structure, nothing but swarms of cadets, some shiny new North American AT 6 training planes, a handful of instructors and Colonel Whitehead. I asked him if he could use a middle-aged infantry reserve officer who was well-acquainted with the people and the suppliers of the Phoenix area. He darned near threw his arms

around me. A week later, I was assigned to one year's active
duty at Luke."

A thirty-one-year-old infantry officer on an Air Force Base
was something like a fish out of water. Barry had been
piloting an airplane when most of the students and many of
the instructors were still in high school, and he had no intention of remaining a chair-born spectator.

It was not difficult to transfer from the Infantry to the
Air Force, but even Colonel Whitehead, who was enthusiastically grateful for Barry's knowledgeable, efficient help,
turned his official thumbs emphatically downward every time
Goldwater expressed his desire to get out of that chair and
into the air. Whitehead and the Air Force failed to take
into account the determined nature of the applicant.

Every hour of time Barry acquired in the AT 6 was boot-
legged, unofficial and strictly against Air Force policy. Barry
just didn't bother to deal directly with the Air Force.

"Every instructor on the base," he says, "wanted pictures
to send home—pictures of them flying, pictures of their airplane, portraits in blouse and cap and wings." Goldwater was
a gifted photographer with all the necessary camera equipment and a private darkroom at home.

That first contingent of instructors at Luke probably became the most photographed group of flying teachers in
the Air Corps, and the price for each print was so much
flying time. Instructors finished their regular classes of students and then flew Goldwater.

"That AT 6 was a well-mannered mother hen compared
to some of the planes I've flown," Barry says, "and after a
few hours of check ride, I got off the ground in one solo. All
told, I logged more than two hundred hours in the Six as
a completely unofficial student."

Barry was home in the house on Manor Drive that Sunday the Japanese attacked Pearl Harbor. All military personnel were ordered to return to their headquarters assignment immediately. Recalling his memories of that morning, Barry says: "It was a horrible thing to listen to the radio and to hear the reports of death and destruction. Yet in one way I experienced a sense of relief. Our reaction would be swift and certain—the uncertainty was ended. Most of us in the training command were aware of the seriousness of the world situation, but the civilian population had not shared our concern. Now it would be different. I believed then and I believe now the people of America will willingly make any sacrifice necessary for the preservation of freedom. We love peace, we prefer to mind our own business; we have no aspirations to enlarge our territory at the expense of our neighbors. Because of all these things, we are sometimes slow to recognize the evil and envy and ambition which influences the actions of other nations."

Barry believes that 1961 has been another year of great awakening for the American people. In regard to the current Communist threat to conquer the world, he maintains that once the American people recognize the extent of the Russian design they will demand that communism be defeated. If the Russians are just clumsy enough to fire one shot in our direction,* there is little likelihood we will be defeated; but if they continue to fool us, to lull us to sleep as they have done so successfully in the last fifteen years, we are in great danger.

When Captain Goldwater was detailed to open a new

---

* Goldwater believes Khrushchev's resumption of atomic testing was a Communist strategic error which may produce a resolute effective response from the American people.

Air Force training school in Yuma, Arizona, in May of 1942, he was still an unofficial pilot in the record books. The opening of the new school required a great deal of travel and time limitations dictated that travel be by air. The Air Force closed its official eye when Captain Goldwater found it convenient and necessary to act as his own pilot on these official trips.

The problems at Yuma were a repetition of those at Luke, only more so. The population of Yuma was about one-tenth that of greater Phoenix and the original assignment brought military personnel equivalent to about half the civilian population, but the birds flew and the cadets became proficient. The community provided all the support the Air Force hoped for, and when the military grudgingly admitted there was a need for experienced older pilots to fly noncombat missions, Goldwater was one of the first to apply for assignment to the new command.

Most of the pilots recruited came into the military service with long experience on commercial lines in various multi-engined aircraft. Barry never had an hour of instruction in a twin-engine airplane. He was sent to a field in Colorado, along with some other pilots, to ferry a group of Cessna UC 78s to Arizona.

"I'd never been in a twin before," Barry says. "I asked somebody how to start the engines and for a briefing on cockpit procedure before I took off. Luckily both fans kept turning. I didn't have the foggiest notion what to do if one of them quit."

Paradoxically, training for multi-engine flying consists almost entirely of flying the multi-engine aircraft with one or more of the engines shut off or throttled back. Any competent pilot can fly a twin-engine aircraft when everything is functioning normally. The single-engine procedures, how to handle the plane when one motor suddenly quits during take-off or landing, constitute the training for this kind of piloting.

After participating in the first and only flight of single-engine fighter planes across the Atlantic, Barry was assigned to the Far Eastern Theatre as Chief Pilot, ATC. The Military Air Transport Service operated constant shuttle flights to all theatres—planes and crews were in the air long hours at a time and the steady, dependable C 54, a military version of the Douglas DC 4, carried the freight. Everything from ammunition to surgical supplies was delivered on time where it was needed.

There was little glamour attached to this service and a good many combat pilots regarded themselves as vastly superior to everyone detailed to these work horse missions.

Barry was stationed at Karachi, India, in 1944, when he received a radiogram which might have ended his military career. The message in typical, terse, Air Force language read: "Report immediately to headquarters. Utilize fastest transportation available."

Headquarters was in New Castle, Delaware. "When I read that message," Barry says, "I thought I was in. They were just getting the heavy bombardment program under way and I'd been trying to get a transfer to multi-engine bombers. The brass had at last come to realize they needed Goldwater's help."

The message caught up with Barry at the British Officer's Club in downtown Calcutta. He had flown in that day from Karachi and the "fastest available transportation" would require him to return to his home base immediately and then continue on to the United States aboard one of the regular transports, via, what he calls, a pony express schedule.

Barry roused the crew that had accompanied him to Calcutta, gassed the airplane and was airborne within an hour. At Karachi the crew was changed, and Goldwater became an extra pilot. The flight stopped for fuel and crew changes in Cairo, Casablanca and the Azores. Three days later Goldwater walked into the command post and saluted.

"Colonel Bowen looked at me like I was a man from Mars."

"What the hell are you doing here, Goldwater?" he demanded.

"I got orders," he told him.

"From whom?"

"You, sir," I said.

"This I want to see."

Fortunately Barry had the crumpled radiogram in his blouse pocket. The colonel read it, read it again, shook his head sadly, and said, "Well, I'll be damned." Then he summoned the communications officer and demanded the sending file. As dispatched from headquarters, the radiogram had been addressed to Major Barry Goldwater, but it read: "Advise Major Crosswell to report headquarters immediately. Use fastest available transportation." The first and most important part of the message had been eliminated by the time it reached Karachi.

"What shall I do?" Goldwater inquired.

"You're not here. Nobody sent for you. You are detailed to Karachi. If I were you I'd get back there as fast as I could." And Barry did. Eighty-five hundred miles back without so much as a twenty-four hour leave in the states, or a stop, or sleep in a regular bunk. "I guess I would have been

court martialled," he says, "if I had not been able to produce
that radiogram."

Barry never was able to effect a transfer to combat duty.
He flew missions across the hump in support of the war in
China; served at different times in every theatre except the
Pacific, and came back to the states a Lt. Colonel in August
of 1944.

When the war was over and Barry was sitting out his discharge attached to the 312th Fighter Training Command in
Glendale, California, time was heavy on his hands. The
pressure of five years of anxiety was suddenly over and
official military discipline became tolerant and understanding. When some of his fellow officers expressed a desire to
see the Smoki dance in Prescott, a convenient excuse was
found for the trip.

Barry was a member of the Smoki Clan, a select group of
white men formed in the early twenties for the purpose of
preserving the beauty and color of Indian religious dances.
At first the Smokis had presented only Hopi ceremonials; in
later years, they have added Navajo and Aztec rituals to
their repertoire. The clansmen dance with live snakes, but,
unlike the Hopis who use the deadly rattler, the Smokis are
content with the harmless bull snake. Once each year in
August the Smoki Clan performs for the public at the fair
grounds. The costumes are authentic, the training is long
and tedious. To be welcomed into the Smoki Clan is to be
truly a citizen of Prescott.

Strangers frequently remark and comment on the blue
dots tatooed on the fleshy part of Goldwater's left hand, the
symbol of membership in the Smokis.

Of course none of these fellow officers would have ever
heard about the Smokis if it had not been for Barry, and

what was a sightseeing junket for them was a chance to return to his native state for Goldwater.

The party was scheduled to fly a B 25 to Nellis Air Force Base in Las Vegas, via Prescott, with a convenient overnight stop to accommodate the tourists. Barry's return to Prescott was regarded as an official homecoming by his fellow Smokis and following the dance they found numerous ways to express their affection. The celebration lasted until daylight and when Goldwater and his party climbed into the B 25, they were exhausted and sleepy.

"That sun looked awfully bright," Barry explained. "So I decided to file an instrument flight plan and go on the gauges. I didn't feel very comfortable squinting through that August sunshine."

This part of the story is probably an exaggeration, but what follows has been verified. Barry, the clothing merchant, has always been extremely conscious of his appearance. When flying it is his habit to take off his coat, or when in uniform-blouse, and place the article on a hanger to preserve the press. Since he had but one pair of uniform trousers with him on this Prescott trip, he decided it would be well to hang up his trousers and fly the thirty-five or forty minutes between Prescott and Las Vegas in his shorts.

Upon arrival over Nellis Air Force Base, military radio granted permission for the landing and gave instructions for taxiing to the transient tie-down area. A jeep was dispatched to bring the visiting officers to headquarters. Barry taxied the B25 into proper position, leaned the engines until they died, cut the switches, and went through the procedures required to close out the flight. Then he slipped into his blouse and climbed down to board the waiting jeep. Before he was settled in the seat, the radio from the jeep blared forth a courteous but urgent request from the control tower.

"Would the Colonel in command of the 25 please put on his trousers before reporting to headquarters!"

CHAPTER X

# BARRY ENTERS PARTISAN POLITICS

MUCH of Arizona is a sizzling furnace in summertime. The normal temperature in the central valleys ranges between 105° and 115°. Each afternoon summer cumulus build their white towers over the mountains, provocatively suggesting the promise of rain, shaking the sky with thunder and stabbing at the earth below with swords of lightning.

The development of refrigerated air conditioning has completely altered the old summer habits. Until the middle 1950s, the end of school was the signal for a general exodus. Mothers and children fled to the mountains and beaches, business activity slowed to a comfortable shuffle and the siesta lasted until the reopening of school, usually the week after Labor Day.

Arizona election laws provide for the selection of candidates by both parties in a statewide primary. The statute calls for the primary election to be held eight weeks in advance of the general election, which usually means a primary election date about mid-September.

Prior to 1950, a victory in the Democratic primary meant certain election. The shortness of the interval between primary and general elections imposed no penalty on candidates eager to get it over with.

The law makers who wanted to make it possible for a maximum number of voters to participate in the primary recognized that any date in advance of school's opening would make it difficult for a great many Arizona citizens to register their primary preferences and to hold a primary at the end of May, would, they believed, leave an awkward interval between the nomination of candidates and the final decision.

In 1950, the Democratic primary produced a mad scramble in the race for Governor—not an unusual situation. The Democratic incumbent was the former Arizona Secretary of State Dan Garvey, who had succeeded to office following the death of Democratic Governor Sidney Osborn. While he had been a good Chief Executive, he didn't control the party machinery, and opposition factions produced two strong primary candidates in Ana Frohmiller, currently the State Auditor, and Richard F. Harless, who had served several terms in the United States House of Representatives. In addition to Garvey, who was running to succeed himself, there were three additional male candidates—Jim Smith, one-time State Senator from Graham County, Howard Sprouse, a perennial candidate, and Ralph A. Watkins, Maricopa County Democratic Party leader.

Party opposition to an incumbent in the primary is not unusual in Arizona. Between statehood in 1912 and 1950, the Republican Party had elected only two Governors—Thomas

E. Campbell in 1918 and John C. Phillips in 1928. The real contests were settled in the primary.

Although badly outnumbered by registered Democrats, Republican candidates in the state had historically received between thirty and forty percent of the ballots cast in the general election. The Republican Party was alive but barely breathing. After eighteen years of Democratic presidents, there were not more than half a dozen appointed or elected officials in the State of Arizona who belonged to the GOP. Old timers in the party knew they were licked before they started. Newcomers did not feel this way. At the spring 1950 meeting of the Republican organization, radio executive Charles Garland, of station KOOL, suggested the party make a determined effort to elect a governor. Garland had been in Arizona only four or five years at the time. He had served as the Republican mayor of Des Plaines, Illinois, and had been the party's candidate for Congress from that state. He did not know enough to realize that a Republican gubernatorial candidate in Arizona was whipped before the race left the starting line.

Garland urged that the party draft forty-three year-old Howard Pyle, a radio personality associated, for many years, with the largest NBC outlet in Arizona, KTAR, as its candidate.

Pyle was young and aggressive, his voice known to thousands of Arizona radio listeners. As creator of the Easter Sunrise broadcast from Grand Canyon, a regular feature on NBC, Pyle had enjoyed statewide newspaper publicity. For years his poetry program had appealed to the sentimental listeners, Republican and Democrat. There was another asset not to be discounted; Pyle had served for a time in the Far East as a war correspondent. He had been present on the

battleship Missouri when Japan surrendered and he made
the luncheon club circuit reciting his war experiences. He
was a good speaker, had a beautiful voice and pleasant smile.
He didn't have any political experience, but where in this
one-party state could you find a candidate on the Republican
side who did?

Colonel Randolph M. J. Evjen, a retired Army chaplain
who had settled in the little city of Florence in Pinal County
and been elected Republican State Chairman, was enthusiastic about Garland's suggestion. In his influential position as
State Chairman he was in a position to do something about it.

Pyle would need a manager—someone widely acquainted
throughout the state—whose sponsorship would lift the Pyle
candidacy out of the category of an ordinary lackadaisical
Republican effort.

Evjen shrewdly canvassed the field of possible campaign
managers and settled on Barry Goldwater—not because Barry
had political experience, but because here was a Republican
who enjoyed the love and respect of men and women in
both parties. Barry had an enviable war record and was in
great demand as a speaker throughout the state.

Evjen believed the old party warhorses could provide the
political experience. Barry had a warm and friendly way
with people. He could think on his feet, express his ideas
clearly, and Evjen hoped that some of Barry's glamour would
rub off on Pyle, who, despite his years before the microphone, presented an image of aloofness which made it difficult for people to know him.

Pyle realized the odds were against his victory in the
gubernatorial campaign, but he had long-term political ambitions. A vigorous effort in 1950 might lay the foundation
for a successful campaign for the United States Senate in

1952, and Pyle was actually more interested in Congress than in the governorship.

Pyle accepted what had begun as a two-man draft and by noon of that day there was a genuine feeling of excitement and enthusiasm emanating from the less than one hundred party stalwarts gathered in the Adams Hotel.

After lunch, Evjen cornered Barry.

"Howard will make a fine candidate," the state chairman argued, "but he needs your help. You can make the difference. People know Howard's name and voice, but they know you personally, and if before this meeting is over you will promise to manage his campaign, the announcement will be like a blood transfusion to the Republican Party of Arizona."

Barry asked for a couple of hours to consider the proposition. Did he want to get into politics? Did he want to enter by this side door? He had enjoyed his years on the city council, but that had been a nonpartisan election. Had they asked him to make the race for Governor, he would have said "yes" in a minute, not primarily from a partisan concern, but because his intimate acquaintance with the state's politics had long ago convinced him that one-party rule was a definite liability for the state and its people.

That afternoon Barry tried repeatedly to contact two of his close friends; neither one could be reached by telephone. Had they been available to give their counsel, it is likely the state's political history might have been different. Both of them were opposed to Barry's becoming involved in the 1950 effort. They felt with the Presidential election coming up in 1952 and with the Democratic incumbent in a position where he probably would not be a candidate for re-election, the odds would favor a Republican winning in Arizona.

From statehood to that date, Arizona had always voted

for the winning presidential candidate. (This record was shattered in 1960 when the state went for Nixon despite Kennedy's victory.)

Barry was intimately acquainted with the political complexion of his native state. He realized that if he accepted the management of the Pyle campaign, and if Arizona politics ran true to form, he must inevitably share some portion of Pyle's defeat.

In other years, Republican candidates had waged milk toast and cracker crumb campaigns, carefully avoiding any frontal assault on the Democratic candidates. Statewide registration was five to one, and even though many of those who registered Democratic voted Republican, it wasn't good business to engage in a bare-knuckle fight. Democrats controlled the courthouses and the statehouse. They played politics to the hilt. No merchant or business man who opposed the Democratic machine could expect any order from county or state governments.

None of these factors had any significant bearing on Barry's decision. What he wanted to know before committing his energies to what might be a forlorn cause was this: did Howard Pyle intend to campaign to win? Or was he planning a repeat performance of past Republican halfhearted efforts?

Evjen, Garland, and National Committeeman, authorjournalist Bud Kelland, all assured Barry that this time the party would go all out. There would be no appeasement, no pulled punches.

Before the concluding dinner meeting, Barry cornered the candidate in a private room. Slight of stature, a little under average height, almost completely bald, with regular features and a pleasant smile, Pyle's natural reserve and meticulous manner of speaking projected dignity. He was an intelligent solid citizen, ten years younger than any of his potential Democratic opponents.

Barry, then forty-one, tall, lean, tanned and handsome, presented a marked contrast to the candidate he had been asked to manage. Where Goldwater was impulsive and daring, Pyle was thoughtful, given to introspection, a man who carefully weighed and examined all the alternatives before reaching a decision.

Goldwater had only one question: "If I take this on, are we going to play for keeps?"

Pyle replied, "With every ounce of determination at my command."

In recent years, Barry has frequently quoted Washington's statement at the Constitutional Convention—"If to please the people we offer what we ourselves disapprove, how can we afterward defend our work? Let us raise a standard to which the wise and honest can repair. The affair is in the hands of God." He accepted Pyle's statement as a declaration of determination and informed Evjen, Garland and Kelland that he would be glad to manage the Pyle campaign.

At this point in his life, articulation of his political beliefs did not come easy to Goldwater. The simple, understandable declaration of faith in the dignity of the individual, and the wisdom of the Constitution, which has attracted supporters from Florida to Oregon, and from California to Maine, was then beyond the ability of this young business man to express. He knew what he believed. He recognized in Pyle a determined comrade in arms. There was work to be done.

Goldwater, whose approach has never been calculating and conniving, was innocent of any of the political guile long associated with Arizona campaigning. The problem, as he viewed it, was to make the face and figure of Pyle as familiar to all the people in Arizona as were the name and the voice.

During the summer months prior to that September primary date, the red, white and blue Bonanza 767-Bravo, with Barry at the controls, carried the two campaigners into every corner of the state. They dodged summer thunderstorms, flew on instruments in bad weather, touched down on metropolitan runways, and slipped into high altitude and hastily-dragged dirt strips of the more remote sections.

Goldwater, to whom flying an airplane has become second nature, held long conversations with his passenger. On these flights between meetings and rallies and visits to the Indian traders, Barry began to spell out the political convictions that are now his trademark. Pyle, who might have been a good deal more cautious if left to his own devices, opened an assault on the entrenched Democratic machine which left his adversaries gasping for breath and caused the more sophisticated politicians in the Republican party considerable concern.

The first big rally was held on a Friday late in August in Glendale, a suburban community ten miles north and west of Phoenix. There were seventeen popular Democrats on the platform, including United States Senator Carl Hayden, who was seeking re-election to the office he'd held since 1927. One observer estimated that eighty percent of the crowd were registered Democrats. Pyle opened by saying:

"Never in my life have I been so glad to be a Republican." Then he began cataloging the failures of the Truman Administration, the bungling and incompetency here at home and the evil of one-party rule. Pyle sympathized with his Democratic friends who found themselves in the grip of a machine which was steadily moving away from the great traditions of the Democratic Party.

The chips were down. Pyle spelled out the Republican conservative philosophy with force and logic. He never spoke meanly of the opposition. He avoided anything which might be construed as personal criticism. He levelled his guns at the underlying philosophy of the party which had ruled the nation since 1932 and Arizona, with few exceptions, since 1912.

Being without Republican opposition in the primary, Pyle could and did devote all of his talents to outlining the benefits which would accrue to Arizona under a Republican Governor.

Despite their valiant efforts, the two campaigners were waging a losing battle. Popular courthouse politicians with their effective political machines could be expected to deliver the Democratic vote. Once the primary battles were over, the party faithful could be expected to join ranks, pull the big lever and snow under the Republican upstart opposition.

Most of the voting places in Arizona are equipped with voting machines on which it is possible to cast a straight party ballot by pulling the Democratic handle. Judges of the Supreme Court and Superior Court appear without party designation. In 1950, there was not a single Republican running for the Supreme Court and only one or two Republicans aspiring to the Superior Court throughout the state.

Political post-mortems occupy the minds and talent of most professional politicians in the period between election years. Defeats are explained with a variety of "ifs." In victory, it is stoutly maintained that superior party organization and superior candidates are responsible for the win. No one ever wants to admit that his man or his party was the beneficiary of a happy circumstance rather than a winner on solid merit and ability. The results of the 1950 Democratic primary still loom enormously in any consideration of Arizona politics. An attractive, middle-aged woman, Ana Frohmiller, who had served with distinction as State Auditor, and in past elections invariably led the ticket, triumphed over her five male opponents and became the Democratic nominee for Governor in the general election.

Other women in other states have been elevated to the post of Chief Executive, and Frohmiller supporters, relying on her proven vote-getting ability, full expected their candidate would be well out in front when the final ballots were counted in November.

Mrs. Frohmiller had an excellent record as a public official. She had received reams of favorable publicity in newspapers as the watchdog of the public treasury. Without regard to partisan politics, Mrs. Frohmiller on many occasions challenged questionable warrants presented to the auditor for payment. In some cases, this action had produced considerable embarrassment for Democratic office holders. Oftentime the amounts involved were trifling and her objections were legalistic and concerned primarily with form and procedure. Even so, most of the people in the state had a sense of admiration and gratitude, coupled with deep respect, for Ana Frohmiller's ability and integrity. This solid public acceptance should have produced a candidacy too strong to be overcome by an upstart radio personality.

Ana Frohmiller was still a woman, despite her ability, her charm and her demonstrated qualifications. The idea of a woman governor was new to Arizona.

Barry sensed a deep-seated reluctance on the part of Republicans and Democrats alike to name a woman Chief Executive.

In the seven counties which had given Ana a majority in the primary, old timers began to shuffle their feet and qualify their predictions.

The candidate herself, accustomed to campaigning in a man's world, overlooked the single asset which might have guaranteed victory. She made no particular appeal for women's votes. There was no organization of women for Frohmiller; there was no militant voice proclaiming equal rights for the fair sex.

As the campaign progressed, Barry wisely counseled Pyle to avoid any reference to the sex of his opponent.

"Be kind, be generous," Barry said. "If you win, victory will come because the male voters of this state just won't go for a woman. But if you make an issue of it, the women will get busy and make this the single issue."

Pyle, who had been only a name and a voice at the beginning of the campaign, was now firmly established as an associate of Barry Goldwater. Under Barry's sponsorship and guidance he had shaken hands with thousands of voters, appeared before dozens of civic groups and been present at political rallys from the Utah border to the Mexican line. Thirty days before election day Republicans accustomed to expecting defeat began to sense that this time the odds were narrowed.

Barry did more than manage his candidate's campaign, he breathed life and vigor into a skeleton party structure. The impact of his determined personality on precinct captains and county chairmen jarred them out of their lackadaisical attitudes. Never before had there been a Republican candidate quite like Pyle; never had there been a campaign like this one.

The Democratic hopefuls toured the state by automobile and caravans. They descended on the little towns and overpowered the locals by sheer weight of numbers. Their first call was always on a county courthouse where Democratic office holders were flattered by the attention they received. Next, the Democrats flipped through the business districts, shaking hands, distributing cards, and behaving much like visiting royalty.

Barry and Howard dropped out of the sky—two young, determined, vigorous crusaders. They shook hands and visited; they were informal. Pyle with his diction and gift of expression outlined and documented the Republican philosophy. Barry, always direct, always friendly, infected the people with his enthusiasm.

Republican Howard Pyle was elected Governor of Arizona on the first Tuesday in November, 1950, by a plurality of 2,991 votes. A miracle had taken place. In a moment of generous honesty, the newly elected Governor credited Barry with the success of the campaign. Actually, the combination of the two of them was the essential ingredient for victory. There are those who still will say that if the Democratic candidate had not been a woman Pyle would still be behind the microphone.

Second guessing is always good fun, but nothing can temper or minimize the finality of the counted ballot. The reasons for victory are relatively unimportant. It's the victory that counts, and in 1950 the modern Republican Party in Arizona was born. Outnumbered then, still outnumbered, the winner perhaps because of a fortuitous circumstance, nevertheless, the GOP was the winner. Governor-elect Pyle offered a recognizable focal point for all the Republican energy within the state. Pyle was in the front seat, but the strength and the muscle and the renewed determination of the rank and file party members belonged to Goldwater.

Pyle, who had secretly hoped to run for the Senate in 1952, suddenly found himself in the Governor's office. Goldwater, whose political perspective had never extended beyond a rather sentimental, indefinite desire to one day be Governor of his native state, had closed the door to this possibility for at least four years.

Following the inauguration ceremony, Barry suffered from that sudden deflationary experience common to all who manage political campaigns. For almost six months every ounce of his ingenuity and energy had been devoted to the cause of Pyle's victory. The candidate had constantly sought his advice. Barry had made almost every political decision. When things went poorly, Barry suffered with the candidate; when the response was enthusiastic and favorable his spirits rode the crest of the waves. The campaign had been a mutual effort, but the day following election the manager becomes excess baggage. The victorious candidate strides alone into the limelight. His words, and his words alone, are sought after. There is no sharing of the victory.

The manager of a baseball team who wins a pennant is a powerful, and often admired, figure. The manager of a successful political campaign usually is forgotten immediately. In defeat, circumstances are reversed. A manager shares the blame and sometimes is given the total credit for the loss. The candidate, who before the election belongs to the party and is totally dependent upon his partisan supporters eagerly seeking and accepting advice, after victory suddenly belongs to the entire electorate.

For Barry this was the first encounter with one of the disillusioning, frustrating aspects of political campaigns. He accepted the situation without complaint, although in later years he said: "As long as Howard Pyle was Governor he never once sought my advice or asked me for a suggestion in connection with the political affairs of the Governor's office."

There was no bitterness in Barry's report, only an indication of a slowly and painfully acquired understanding of an ancient political fact. The candidate sits in the front seat. After election day, managers and finance chairmen and publicity experts are usually treated as excess baggage.

The amazing display of Republican strength was dismissed as nothing more than a combination of fortunate circumstance, but to the members of the Republican Party in Arizona it had greater significance. They had learned that hard work and effective leadership, the kind Barry had displayed, plus a candidate with an attractive personality, could overcome the registration odds.

Barry took a long vacation and then turned his attention toward 1952. Pyle was certain to be the party's gubernatorial candidate. McFarland, the incumbent Democratic U.S. Senator who would come up for re-election in 1952, was considered his party's most able vote getter. But President Truman was beginning to lose his popularity; McFarland was an Administration Senator who had gone down the line with the Fair Deal. More and more the big brother welfare state was invading the life of the individual, and this usurpation of power must some day be challenged for the good of the Republic.

Barry, who had never been awed by the odds against him, began to think about next time.

CHAPTER **XI**

## "NOW IS THE TIME"

BARRY opened his formal general election campaign for the United States Senate in Prescott, Arizona, on September 18, 1952. The selection of Prescott was a concession to sentiment. It was here that Big Mike had finally lowered his roots through the granite rock of Arizona and established a permanent headquarters for the Goldwaters' commercial venture. Prescott had been the original territorial capital, and although Barry had been born in the house on Central Avenue in Phoenix, Prescott was his spiritual birthplace.

The city, like the granite hills surrounding it, is solid and ancient and in many respects stern and uncompromising.

The courthouse, a three-story stone structure topped by the county jail, is located in the center of town on a square block surrounded by elms and grass and flowers. In the plaza square is the heroic equestrian statue of Bucky O'Neil, recruiter and captain of the Rough Riders, who rode up San

Juan Hill behind Teddy Roosevelt and gave his life to purchase freedom for the Cubans.

Much of the square is paved with concrete, and since this is a public building designed and erected at the turn of the century, access to the main floor is gained by climbing a breathtaking flight of stone steps.

To the west of the plaza stands Whiskey Row, tamed and subdued and incredibly drab now that modern niceties have banned the painted women and left only the shell of a block, where once every establishment catered to the rough pleasures of the frontier.

The internal combustion engine, the rubber tire, and the asphalt pavement advancing beneath the banner of progress have banished the hitching rails and the cowboys' straight-necked quarter horses. But on a Saturday night the majority of the customers still cling to their high-heeled boots, the tops concealed beneath the uniform of the West cut out of blue denim by Levi Strauss.

Due north of the plaza is a solid phalanx of two and three-story structures. Here the Bashford-Burmister General Store once supplied the needs of a frontier area larger in size than the state of New Jersey. On the second floors of these buildings, frontier lawyers in black coats and string ties prepared their cases for court. In one of these offices, in 1914, Jimmy Douglas put together the combination of copper claims which became "The Little Daisy" and paid out more than a hundred million dollars in profits.

To the east of the plaza stands the foreboding, ugly building of the First National Bank of Arizona. No welcome here for the would-be borrower. The solid native stone and the uncompromising, drab interior speak eloquently of hard-headed management and deposited treasures in safe keeping.

Southeast is the aging brick building which housed on its lower floor the Goldwater store, and on the second story the first Masonic Lodge in the territory.

On the night of September 18, 1952, no one paid any attention to the buildings or the memories lurking in attic and window. Three hundred folding chairs were set up on a concrete apron in front of the main steps on the Gurley Street side. The area was lighted with a few bare bulbs. At the top of the steps there was an improvised podium. The crowd gathered early; there were not nearly enough chairs to go around. Lean-faced cowboys stood comfortably on the grass. Youngsters annoyed their mothers with incessant "whys." At exactly eight o'clock, with microphones open to every NBC affiliate-transmitter in the state, a forty-three year old ladies ready-to-wear merchant, with a pioneer family name and a vast reservoir of inexperience, challenged the most powerfully entrenched political figure in the state.

Election campaigns have been dissected and second guessed and researched by all sorts of experts—some qualified, some totally inept.

Was it the issue or the personality? Was it merely a case of a candidate being in the right place at the right time? Or does the outcome justify our faith in the machinery of self-government as established in this Democratic Republic?

Many candidates have seen their ambitions destroyed as a result of a single campaign. A thoughtless mistake, an unavoidable blunder, a flip word uttered in jest has spelled oblivion.

Others successful in their initial ventures have been haunted by charges of dirty politics; by whispers within their own party of disloyalty to the rest of the ticket. In the case of Richard Nixon, the Voorhees and Douglas contests, which saw him triumphant over these darlings of the Liberal set, produced a continued reaction which exerted more influence over his 1960 Presidential effort than did his advisors and counselors. The efforts of John Kennedy, in the West Virginia and Wisconsin primaries, with a powerful steam roller combining ruthless political brains and unlimited financial resources, flattened the hopes of Hubert Humphrey.

Most men in public office today can look back upon campaign statements which would have been better left unsaid and campaign promises which could never be fulfilled. A politician is not measured in inches or weighed in pounds. His stature is determined by the dimensions of his campaign efforts and the honesty of his campaign promises.

In the market place, men seek to buy dreams and hopes and anticipation, accepting only as much reality as is necessary to answer the pressing demands of the moment. Politicians and political candidates are forever caught between what the world is and what man hopes it might be. The candidacy of Barry Goldwater was compounded of both dreams and reality. This dashing young man was in a very real sense a knight in shining armor. The reality of his accomplishments gave genuine substance to the position of affection he had earned in the hearts of his fellow citizens.

It was no ordinary political crowd which gathered on the plaza at Prescott that evening. Of the more than twelve hundred people, less than four hundred were members of the candidate's Republican Party. Many of them had been attracted by the almost breathtaking audacity of the young man in the severely-tailored business suit who had undertaken to accomplish the impossible.

It can be argued that 1952 was no ordinary year in American politics. President Harry Truman's popularity had suffered greatly because of the Korean War fiasco and the parade of scandalous revelations revolving around White House figures and Truman cronies. But Arizona had voted for Truman in 1948 and whatever else he may have lacked, Harry was a courthouse politician who knew how to reward his friends and solidify their loyalty. This was truly a battle of David against Goliath and the plaza crowd had been attracted primarily by curiosity, though there were some who had come because of a warm, personal feeling for the audacious young man.

Most of Uncle Morris' old cronies were resting comfortably beneath headstones in the cemetery or living in a world of memories as guests of the state's Pioneer Home. Morris had closed the Prescott store in the early thirties, and although Barry had reopened a retail outlet in the mountain city, the Goldwater name had more sentimental attachment than political significance.

In view of all that has transpired since that September evening, the words of Barry's opening campaign speech assume new significance. *The New York Times* and the Washington *Post* and the many liberal journalists who have attempted to categorize Goldwater as the man opposed to everything since running water, will blindly refuse to remember that this Republican, who has become the conservative leader of the United States, opened his campaign with a tribute to the concepts of certain social measures which are inseparably linked to Franklin D. Roosevelt's New Deal.

He said, "Let me speak directly to all sincere men and women who are concerned with retaining the social gains which have been made in the past twenty years.

"This nation along with the rest of the world went through a depression twenty years ago. You haven't forgotten it, I haven't forgotten it, and every New Deal spokesman reminds us of it in every Fair Deal speech.

"Out of the struggle and misery of those years we found an answer to certain problems.

"We found a method of regulating the trading of securities which serves to help protect the individual investor.

"We established our new system of social security and unemployment insurance, and old-age assistance, aid to dependent children and to the blind.

"We established the FHA to make long-term financing available for home purchasers.

"These things have been a great benefit to the people. They were created by the Congress of the United States and no responsible Republican and especially not this Republican has any intention or desire to abolish any one of them."

Then elaborating on the concept of that ancient Greek who said, "Every good and perfect institution has within itself the seeds of its own destruction through an excess of its own virtue," Barry catalogued the recent failures of these programs to meet the objective for which they were established.

He called the attention of the audience to the lax and slipshod operation of the FHA as administered under Truman cronies.

No promises were implied or expressed. It was a sober, thoughtful indictment of the failure of the Democratic administration to make its programs produce the benefits they might produce with more efficient administration.

Goldwater referred to his opponent, McFarland, as the Junior Senator. It should be noted that the Junior Senator was then Majority Leader of the Senate with twelve years seniority, the personal spokesman for Harry Truman and a courthouse politician who had graduated from County Attorney to Judge, then to the U.S. Senate.

Barry devoted three pages of that speech to the presidential contest. He commented that all of Arizona had heard his opponent introduce the Fair Deal Presidential aspirant to an Arizona audience.

"The Junior Senator," Barry said, "described his candidate as a man possessing the courage of Andrew Jackson and the wisdom of Woodrow Wilson. He neglected to add that his candidate was also the personal choice of Harry Truman and won the nomination only after Harry made his personal power evident.

"The Junior Senator will not tell you his candidate had long and expensive training in the principles of personal government so dear to the heart of Harry Truman. He didn't tell you his candidate commenced government service in the unconstitutional NRA Administration and studied foreign policy under Dean Acheson.

"We have some strange and wonderful situations in this campaign," he commented. "We have Governor Stevenson saying there is a mess in Washington, but Harry Truman says he knows of no mess.

"We have Governor Stevenson saying the Communists have been driven out of government, but Harry Truman says the investigation of Communists was only a red herring."

Barry's opponent, McFarland, in a moment of political exuberance, had described himself to the press as one of the four most powerful men in Washington, and Barry had no intention of letting his audience forget this display of ego.

"Standing in this exalted position," Barry demanded, "does the Junior Senator accept twenty-five percent of the responsibility for James P. Finnigan, St. Louis collector of internal revenue, who has been convicted of misconduct?

"Does the Junior Senator accept twenty-five percent of the responsibility of James A. Mullally, the Justice Department's criminal lawyer who took a gift of $750 from a law firm representing a defendant in a government case?

"Does the Junior Senator accept twenty-five percent of the responsibility of William M. Boyle, Jr. or five percenter Johnny Maragon, or White House Assistant Donald Dawson?

"Will the Junior Senator from Arizona take twenty-five percent credit for increasing your taxes—for the fact that the federal government is collecting eight-hundred percent more in taxes than was collected in 1941?"

It was a slashing attack and the faint-hearted who read this will say the speech was unfair. We can expect them now to climb to the battlements and raise the cry of McCarthyism and guilt by association. But in this case the subject of the attack had claimed the association and boasted that he was one of the four most powerful men in government, therefore, he must be given twenty-five percent of the credit for the accomplishments of the Truman Administration; and if he was to take the credit, Barry intended to see to it he would also share the criticism.

There are observers who believe the Senate campaign was decided in the final five minutes of Barry's speech that night. McFarland, in a moment of utter candor, speaking to what he regarded as a friendly audience in his home county of Pinal, had made a statement about the Korean War which was relayed to Barry by the friend who met him at the airport. McFarland's statement had shocked and sickened Barry. Now he departed from his prepared statement to share with every Arizona citizen within the sound of a radio loudspeaker both the callous pronouncement and the fighting rage of a man who has suddenly seen something dear and cherished pushed into the gutter.

McFarland, who had opened his own campaign in Casa Grande, Arizona, with the assistance of Speaker Sam Rayburn, had announced that he would ignore this gadfly opposition, and in his apparent desire to express contempt for his upstart Republican opponent, had refused to argue what Goldwater regarded as the paramount issues—peace, individual freedom, and the increasing size and power concentrated in big government, big business and big labor.

Barry called attention to McFarland's reluctance to take a stand on any issue, and now as he threw aside his manuscript and lowered his voice to keep from revealing his indignation. He repeated the message, which had been given to him verbally at first and then verified in writing.

"My opponent who has been so silent on so many things has spoken out on one subject within this past week. You are entitled to know what he said. In Coolidge, Arizona, this Junior Senator, speaking to a service club, described our Korean War as a cheap war. Cheap, he said, because we're killing nine Chinese for every American boy. And then to justify his participation in this blunder of the Truman Administration, he added to his statement these words: 'It is the Korean War which is making us prosperous.'

"I challenge the Junior Senator from Arizona," Barry demanded, "to find anywhere within the borders of this state, or within the borders of the United States, a single mother or father who counts our casualties as cheap—who'd be willing to exchange the life of one American boy for the nine Communists or the nine hundred Red Communists, or nine million Communists."

A candidate of less sincerity, one more skilled in the manipulation of human emotions, would very likely at this juncture have referred to his own personal record of service in World War II. It is indicative of Barry's attitude towards his own accomplishments that it never occurred to him to cite those words which most politicians roll around in their mouth like honeyed biscuits—"I know war for I've served—I've seen men die on the battlefield, etc."

It never occurred to Barry, a colonel in the Air Force Reserve with a service record extending around the world, to make mention of this. Instead, he just said: "Now is the time to reaffirm our devotion to those moral principles of honesty, integrity, and justice. Now is the time for faith; faith in our own ability; faith in the power of truth; faith in Almighty God; and faith in man's destiny as a child of freedom with God-given freedom of choice; free to choose good over evil, truth over falsehood and peace over war."

The campaign issues were joined.

CHAPTER **XII**

## "BARRY CAN'T WIN"

PUBLIC curiosity immediately fastens on a man whose ability and achievements mark him as being somehow different from his fellows. This is particularly true in our attitude toward public figures. We probe and analyze and dissect them with the revealing spotlight of publicity.

It is never easy to arrive at a simple understanding of why certain men behave in a certain fashion. Edmund Burke has said it is the diversity between men which makes society viable and progress possible. The truth of Burke's observation is underscored by the attitude of those who direct our channels of mass communication. Newspapers give headlines to the misbehavior of man. Controversy and disagreement, particularly when accompanied by violence, makes news. The unexpected is always treated in twenty-four point bold face type.

"Spectacular, unusual, bold, daring, unconventional, wild

and uninhibited"—all these words have been used by newspaper writers and commentators in an attempt to identify
and classify the characteristics which make Barry Goldwater
different.

Up to this point in his lifetime he had done all the ordinary
things which make up the total of most men's lives: grammar
school, high school, college, marriage and fatherhood. Yet
these prosaic experiences were altered somehow, lifted out
of the ordinary by the impact of Goldwater's personality.

He is in many ways a contradictory figure. He has a low
boiling point and at the same time a greater degree of tolerance than most of his fellows. He is both quixotic and extremely practical, bold and cautious. He attracts attention
without meaning to attract attention. Extremely sophisticated
in many ways, he is at the same time dangerously naïve in
his attitude toward those out to destroy him.

Following the inauguration of President Kennedy, Barry
was asked to appear on a television panel with Secretary of
Labor Arthur Goldberg. Throughout the program Goldberg
constantly made invidious references to Goldwater's wealth,
motives and doctrinaire conservatism.

Immediately following the broadcast Barry telephoned me
and asked my reaction. When I expressed my disapproval of
Goldberg's attitude, Barry's reply was, "Steve, you've got to
meet this guy. You would like him. He's intelligent, capable
and completely genuine. There is nothing phony about his
attitude. Of course I don't agree with him, but you would
like him."

When Barry Goldwater became a candidate for the United
States Senate, this action was newsworthy. Barry was not a
politician. His entrance into the political contest was unan-
ticipated. His fellow Arizonans knew him as an aggressive

young business man, prominent in civic, cultural and charitable activities; a romantic figure with a record of successes, from exploring the unknown regions of the Colorado River to documenting Arizona's case against California for usurping the precious resources of that stream.

If a preacher had renounced his pulpit to play the piano in a saloon, the community would likely have responded with the same degree of shock and eager interest it displayed when Barry announced, as a Republican, he would oppose Ernest McFarland.

It is probable that Barry's entrance into politics was inevitable. Big Mike and Joe and Uncle Morris during their lifetimes had all been candidates. Morris was one of the founders of the Democratic Party in Arizona. The Goldwater family was inseparably linked to the development of this desert land. It would have been out of character for Barry to remain aloof from the responsibilities of government.

In territorial days and in the early years of statehood, particularly prior to 1932, private social and economic organizations exerted far greater influence on the life of the individual than did government. With the great depression and subsequent concentration of power in Washington, political decisions began to make their impact on almost every area of individual living.

In 1936, following Franklin Delano Roosevelt's re-election, Barry expressed his concern over what, to him, were the fundamental failures of the welfare state concept in a letter to the editor of *The Arizona Republic*. The letter was widely quoted in editorials throughout the state, because of its logic and because of the prominence of its author. A business man commenting on politics was as freakish as a two-headed calf.

By 1952, almost everyone had forgotten this early protest on behalf of individual dignity.

The people of Arizona in that year were still enjoying the close relationships common to the western frontier. They took their politics seriously, and when a citizen said, "I know so-and-so and I'm going to vote for him," he meant exactly what he said. A candidate's personal acquaintance was his greatest asset and if large enough could assure his victory.

Arizona voters registered by party; in 1952 the 330,083 voters preferred the Democratic Party in a ratio of about five to one.

Ernest McFarland had a wide personal acquaintance. He was an affable, friendly fellow who had commenced his political career as County Attorney, graduated to Superior Court Judge, and then won election to the Senate in 1940 over a fellow Democrat, incumbent Henry Ashurst.

Ashurst had served in the Senate since statehood. He was an orator of the old school, addicted to coats which suggested the Prince Albert, a senatorial haircut, and, whenever possible, seven syllable words.

Henry had been a good Senator and in other years a good campaigner. In 1939 and 1940, as Chairman of the Senate Judiciary Committee, Ashurst had recognized what most Americans refused to believe—the inevitability of our involvement in the European conflict. His continued presence in Washington, although not required, was highly desirable, and Ashurst was more loyal to the responsibilities of the nation than to his own political future. He did not come home to campaign until two weeks before the primary election.

In the meantime, Ernest McFarland was hard at work. As a visiting Superior Court Judge, he had presided in most of

United States Senator Barry Goldwater

Big Mike Goldwater, Barry's grandfather

Sarah Nathan Goldwater, wife of Big Mike, Barry's grandmother

Josephine Williams Goldwater, Barry's mother, in her nurse's uniform, taken at about the time she was married to Baron Goldwater

Baron Goldwater, Barry's father

*Howey's Building ~ Prescott*

The Goldwater Store at Prescott, Arizona, as it originally appeared

Barry Goldwater during his school days

The Goldwater family, left to right seated: Barry Goldwater, Jr.; Senator Barry Goldwater; Mrs.

Barry Goldwater with Dwight D. Eisenhower during their 1952 campaigns

Barry Goldwater at Luke Field, Arizona

In the cockpit

Barry Goldwater with his plane, the Peggy G.

On active duty: Senator (Colonel then, now Brigadier General)
Barry Goldwater of Arizona is being greeted by Brig. Gen. William
E. Eubank and Col. Sam Byerley at Castle Air Force Base, Cali-
fornia

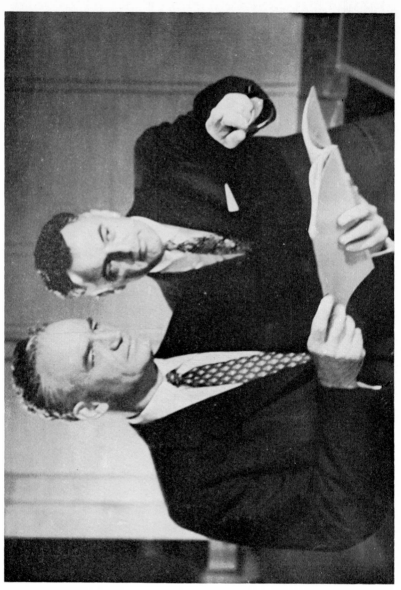

Stephen Sherlock with Brewer Goldsmith

Stephen C. Shadegg, author of this book

Freedom is His Flight Plan

176

the county seats throughout the state. He was acquainted with the courthouse politicians, and he waged an unusual, but singularly effective, campaign. Issues were not discussed. There was no criticism of the action or voting record of Senator Ashurst.

McFarland's appeal for support boiled down to this one simple question: How long has it been since you have seen our Senior Senator?

Ashurst had last actively campaigned for his seat in 1934. He had been home in 1936 and 1938, but much of his time in the state had been occupied with official business which did not bring him into contact with a great number of voters.

McFarland won the primary, and the results of the general election were a foregone conclusion. In defeat, Ashurst established a permanent residence in Washington. The dowagers of the capital city are still an admiring audience for his learned lectures.

McFarland never misinterpreted the results of that first election: "out of sight, out of mind" was the slogan which had opened the gates of glory. He had no intention of permitting the same fate to happen to him. During the war it was difficult for Senators to spend much time in their home state. Congress was constantly in session, but McFarland kept his political fences in order. He came home frequently, and when at home he visited every county. He may have missed some votes in the Senate, but he did not miss many voters in Arizona. His re-election in 1946 had been a walkaway.

In 1949, when the Democrats regained control of the Congress, McFarland was elevated to the position of majority leader. His enemies insisted he was a compromise candidate, chosen because he was affable and pliable. Insiders claimed that he was Harry Truman's personal choice, an outgrowth of their friendly association in the Senate. Whatever the reason, he was elected Majority Leader, a position of power not usually given to a Senator from a sparsely populated frontier state.

In 1950 Arizona's Senior Senator Carl Hayden had disposed of his primary opposition and gone on to win re-election over a likeable and energetic Republican candidate, Bruce Brockett, by a margin of more than 47,400 votes. Of the two men, McFarland was considered the far better vote-getter.

With this background in political history it is easy to understand why most Arizonans refused to take Barry's candidacy for the Senate seriously.

McFarland's personal reaction was probably that of a crown prince suddenly challenged by a bastard peasant from some far-off corner of the realm. He regarded Barry as a nice young boy who was doing fairly well with the ready-to-wear store he had inherited, but certainly no serious threat in the area of politics. In fact, Barry's effrontery produced among McFarlandites an angry annoyance. They didn't worry about the outcome; Barry couldn't win. The people, and particularly those individuals quoted in the newspapers as competent observers of the political scene, agreed unanimously with McFarland.

Aside from the discovery of gold, the most significant factor in the development of our western territories was the construction of the transcontinental railroad. When the Southern Pacific tracks reached Tucson, in southern Arizona, on March 20, 1880, local pride vented its joy and enthusiasm in a three-day commemoration. Some individuals suggested

to the town fathers that it would be proper to wire the Pope
and ask his blessing on the event.

A cable was sent. Some impudent practical joker took it
upon himself to reply, and a faked answer was received
which read: "Most happy to bless the coming of the railroad
to Tucson, Arizona. But where in the hell is Tucson?"

In 1952, most of the residents of Arizona echoed the sentiment of that wacky telegram. Goldwater was welcome to run,
but in politics who in the hell was Goldwater?

As a boy, Barry, who was not a gifted athlete, made up
for this with enthusiasm and determination sufficient to earn
him a place on the team. He came out of college with a
permanent knee injury and the admiration of his competitors.
When he entered the merchandising field, he devoted every
ounce of energy and ability to mastering the complexities of
the store. When Peggy gave him a camera for his birthday,
he lost himself in this hobby and developed such a talent that
he was accepted in the Royal Photographic Society of London. His Indian pictures and studies of the old West have
been collected into two volumes, now out-of-print and extremely valuable.

When the Colorado River controversy suddenly became
hot as the result of a chronic water shortage turned acute,
Goldwater became one of the most knowledgeable men on
this subject. He is still remembered for his service on the
Arizona Interstate Stream Commission and recognized as
an authority on one of the most complex tangles ever produced in the West.

His friends agree Barry has never been interested super-
ficially in anything. If a subject or activity enlisted his interest it became, for the time being at least, all engrossing.

There is more here than just the acceptance of the old

admonition that if a thing is worth doing, it is worth doing well. It is impossible for Barry to be a spectator. Other men give passive acquiescence to concepts and projects. Goldwater must make a passionate affirmation, must become a participant regardless of the effort or personal sacrifice involved.

Had Ernest McFarland been aware of this characteristic in his opponent, he probably would not have been so optimistic in 1952. If the people of Arizona had understood this rock-hard aspect of the Republican candidate, their attitude toward the David and Goliath contest would certainly have been different. Such an understanding might have altered the outcome. Overconfidence has been responsible for many a major political upset.

Goldwater was a Republican identified with management. Certain labor union bosses automatically opposed his candidacy. Their resolve to bring about his defeat was strengthened because Barry had been a strong supporter of the right-to-work law, which was first adopted in Arizona in 1940. This early union-boss opposition did not carry the frenzied hatred generated in 1958, but Barry chose to meet it head on at almost the very beginning of his first major political contest.

His habit of confronting his opposition in person is still most disconcerting to his organized enemies who appear to prefer secondhand or hearsay estimates of the Goldwater position and political philosophy.

Barry, who is extremely cordial to newspaper reporters even when they ask questions designed to produce embarrassment, displays resentment only when an inaccurate statement appears, authored by some writer who made no effort to secure personal verification of the facts.

In 1961 the respected *New York Times* ran a profile on Goldwater, containing both praise and criticism. Barry didn't object to the criticism, but he boiled when the *Times* published some inaccuracies in regard to his book *The Conscience of a Conservative* and the newspaper column *How Do You Stand, Sir?* * His reaction was typically Goldwater.

"If the *Times* wanted the truth, all they had to do was telephone me. I would have told them."

Barry, who has never side-stepped a hot question or ducked a controversial issue, tackled the union-boss opposition in 1952 by securing an invitation to appear before a conference of union officials and management representatives.

With what students of practical politics classify as alarming candor, Barry laid it on the line.

He told these two natural antagonists that any continuation of provoked or artificial conflict between management and labor was wrong. He insisted that a citizen's first concern must be for the total welfare of all the people.

"It is because of our common concern with these problems that you and I are here tonight," he said. "Along with all your other concerns, you have a special interest in discovering just where I stand on certain issues.

"In this land we have made tremendous strides in technical skill, in production and engineering practices, and in scientific knowledge. We have come a long way from the twelve hour work day, the seven day week and the two dollar pay scale. We have come this far in the memory of one man's lifetime, and we don't propose to go back.

---

* Cabell Phillips, in a byline story of June 30, 1961, generously credited Stephen Shadegg with writing Goldwater's book *The Conscience of a Conservative*. The statement is not true.

"Yet there are reckless, irresponsible forces in this land today, seeking to serve themselves by exploiting a difference which actually does not exist.

"There are those eager to magnify every discussion between management and labor into a full-scale battle. They profit politically by creating one crisis after another. They have been successful at the expense of real progress.

"We are all familiar with the demagogue who stirs up management to make reckless charges against labor.

"We quickly recognize the irresponsible labor leader who makes reckless charges against management."

The steel mills were on strike at the time and Barry pulled no punches in discussing this touchy situation.

"We have in this nation the sorry spectacle of a general strike against the great steel producing mills. We have heard accusation and counter-accusation. Each side has offered proof of the validity of its position. I would suggest to you tonight that, in this steel strike, both management and labor are wrong; wrong because they are permitting this controversy to continue. When we sweep aside the screen of hypocrisy and self-interest, we must conclude that both management and labor have the same objective.

"What is good for management is good for labor, and what is good for labor is good for management, because real progress in America has been the result of the fifty-fifty contribution made by management and labor working as a team.

"Big business has been the whipping boy for those who seek to promote their own ends by arousing passion and prejudice. You and I know that, in many instances, big business has deserved everything which has been said against it.

"It was these abuses practiced in big business which gave

us the Sherman Anti-Trust Act and other beneficial legislation to curb and control those segments of big business which
are governed by selfish motives.

"And I would like to add that much of the credit for the
correction of these abuses belongs to organized labor. In the
past twenty-five years we have seen the pendulum swing the
other way. We have seen some unions and some union leaders become as arbitrary and as self-serving as were the robber
barons of big business during their period of ascendancy.
Yet, fundamentally, there is no cleavage; there can be no
cleavage between management and labor."

Then he concluded by saying:

"No man can be a friend of labor without being also a
friend of management. And when two of your friends have
mutual problems, you don't stand between them, you walk
forward with them toward a solution of those problems.

"You will never find me standing on the fence between
management and labor. You'll always find me ready to march
forward with management and labor toward higher wages,
better working conditions, improved job security, toward a
reasonable and proper return on capital, and toward that
goal which is in the heart of every American, the mainte-
nance of freedom, recognition of the integrity and importance of the individual, and the social, economic, moral and
spiritual progress of this land we love."

In the speech there was no pussy-footing, no appeal for
votes, no compromise or partisanship. In his opinion, management and labor must be working partners expressing
toward each other a mutual respect.

"Bad politics," said the professionals.

"He won't side with us," said the union bosses.

"He's taking labor's part," said management.

But the people who were to vote in the 1952 election, those who labored in management and those who labored with the tools, heard and understood.

CHAPTER **XIII**

## THE PEOPLE UNDERSTOOD

**W**HEN Roland Bibolet, Senator McFarland's administrative assistant and close personal adviser, was asked to explain his boss' defeat in the 1952 election, he recited the following lines:

> "Mac is for Harry
> Harry's all through
> You be for Barry
> 'Cause Barry's for you."

There was a fifth line—Goldwater for Senator—and the five-line jingle, spaced like Burma Shave signs, adorned most of the highways of Arizona during the forty days preceding the 1952 general election.

Bibolet's explanation was, of course, over-simplification. Yet in a very real sense it expresses the reason for McFarland's upset. Goldwater campaigned against the Truman

Administration, and because McFarland was so closely linked with the actions of the President from Missouri, he found himself serving as the available target for citizen resentment against the Truman scandals.

The jingle signs, which Bibolet credited with spelling the difference between victory and defeat, caused Barry's only explosion of temper during the campaign.

It was necessary to send someone around to predetermined locations to put up the "Burma Shave" signs. Installing two hundred sets of five-line jingles is quite an undertaking. On high-speed highways, each line was spaced three hundred feet apart; on slower roads the signs were closer together. The jingles had been lettered on what is known in the trade as sign cloth, an inexpensive fabric similar to oil cloth, and then glued to cheap one-by-eight pine boards five feet long. The boards, in turn, were bolted to steel fence posts which could easily be driven into the ground. To conserve dwindling campaign cash a volunteer was entrusted with this assignment. Barry provided a 1948 green Chevrolet which he had used for camping and exploration trips and affectionately referred to as "The Green Dragon."

The volunteer, who was well-intentioned but unfortunately absent-minded, forgot to have the oil checked, and the engine literally burned up in a remote section of the state one hundred and fifty miles from Phoenix. When the news was relayed to Barry, he exploded. No mule skinner ever described the arbitrary obstinacy of these renowned quadrupeds in more colorful or descriptive language than Goldwater used. Then he sent the volunteer a telegram thanking him for what he was doing and completely ignoring the destruction of his cherished "Green Dragon."

Washington observers, who still pretend to be mystified

over what makes Goldwater tick, could find an easy solution to their puzzle by studying the records of that first Goldwater campaign.

On May 31, 1952, William Mathews, Democratic editor and publisher of the *Tucson Daily Star,* asked in his lead editorial, "What kind of a Republican are you, Mr. Goldwater?"

Barry replied in a letter to the editor and in a radio speech to the people of Arizona.

"I am not a 'me too' Republican.

"I am not a 'Fair Deal' Republican.

"I am a Republican who believes all Republicans and all Democrats must practice in their personal and business lives those principles of honesty, integrity, devotion and thrift which all of us long to see reestablished in our national government.

"I am a Republican opposed to the super-state's gigantic, centralized authority, whether it be administered by Democrats or Republicans.

"I am a Republican opposed to communism and particularly to the Communist-inclined sympathizers and Communist-inclined policy-makers and their companion wishful thinkers.

"I am a Republican who gives more than lip service to a balanced budget. I believe individuals and local governments, city councils, county supervisors and state legislatures must reassert their independence and their responsibility; that we, the free people of this nation, must demand an end to government subsidies, deficit financing and living beyond our income.

"I am a Republican who believes we must practice economy in regard to our own projects, and I am a Republican who believes economy must be had in respect to the national budget.

"I am a Republican who believes that management and labor must work together, who refuses to recognize a separation of goals and objectives between management and labor.

"I am a Republican who believes that free men, working freely together, free of the coercion of federal bureaucratic interference and the compulsion of high federal tax demands, can and will work out their own salvation.

"I am a Republican who has a profound respect for those principles of individual responsibility and limitation of the power of the central government first expressed by Thomas Jefferson and now ignored by the Fair Dealers and the New Dealers, who have usurped control of the Democratic Party.

"I am a Republican who believes that man's freedom comes from Almighty God; that man possesses an important human integrity and an immortal soul; that man can never achieve his highest capacities except in a climate of individual freedom."

Senator Barry Goldwater, who in 1959 demanded that his party refuse to perpetuate a dime-store version of the New Deal, remains true to the statements of candidate Goldwater answering Mr. Mathews' question.

The freshman Republican Senator from Arizona, who on the Senate floor condemned the budget demands of a Republican President, was certainly consistent with the candidate who spoke to the people of Arizona in the fall of 1952, when he said:

"The federal budget covers twelve hundred printed pages and weighs approximately ten pounds, and that's a lot of budget.

"Committees of Congress are set up to review and examine

these proposed expenditures. I doubt if any one man in Congress, or any one man in the administration, possesses anything like a clear understanding of the federal budget, and I'm certain that I don't understand it.

"I do understand this. The federal budget, as advanced by Mr. Truman, is an administration budget, looping together the financial demands of thousands of federal agencies and bureaus.

"And when anyone raises his voice to question any one of these items the immediate answer is: 'Well, you tell us where to cut it.'

"I would suggest in general that the proof of necessity must be placed squarely on the spenders and not on the savers."

In that campaign, Goldwater never tempered his words to produce a favorable reaction from his listeners. Sometimes it was difficult to determine if he was campaigning for Barry Goldwater or Dwight Eisenhower.

As a member of the United States Senate, Goldwater has steadfastly opposed expansion of the bureaucratic central state which our federal government has become. Campaigner Goldwater, on October 27, 1952, speaking to an audience composed almost entirely of members of the Democratic Party in Douglas, Arizona, said these words:

"Now is the time for a return to those basic principles of individual enterprise and individual freedom which were the foundation for the development of the mining industry in our state.

"It is this freedom of action—free men seeking to work out their own destiny which pushed back the western frontiers. It will be free men working in concert toward the objective of world peace, of solid prosperity, and the continuation of freedom which gives hope to the future.

"What is the avowed objective of all the planners of the super-state? They attract your sympathy and support by voicing their devotion to the improvement of man's lot in this imperfect world. They cry out against all the abuses of the past and they say—give us the power over your lives and we will correct these abuses by compulsion.

"They point to all of man's past failures and they say—give us the power to regulate your lives and we will correct all the failures of the past.

"They say—think as we think, believe what we tell you to believe, obey our orders, and you have nothing to worry about.

"I deny and reject their claim, for they would trade us slavery for freedom, dependence for individual liberty and make free men subjects of government.

"My friends, government can never make men free or happy or prosperous. Government in and of itself cannot even make the world a peaceful world. Government can not make the world a prosperous world. Your future and my future and the future of our children is dependent not upon the actions of the super-state, but upon the actions of the individuals who make up our political, social and economic society.

"You and I are concerned with the menace of Communism. You and I are concerned every time the lamp of freedom goes out somewhere in our allegedly free world.

"If we are to preserve the benefits of freedom, we must, as individuals, be directly and actively concerned with poverty, with hunger and with disease wherever it occurs and threatens the individual human being.

"The progress of mankind, my friends, is measured in the acts of man-to-man charity and person-to-person justice performed on an individual basis, motivated by the desire of the free individual to serve his God and to love his fellow men.

"Political governments are only the expression of what the individual citizen is willing to tolerate or is willing to support by his labor, his allegiance and his substance.

"Let us then, in this fall of 1952, rededicate ourselves to the cause of liberty, to the perpetuation of justice, to the end of intolerance, toward the creation of a society where love shall outweigh hate, where justice shall defeat bigotry and equality shall end discrimination, where all men shall have a new birth in freedom under Almighty God."

Reserve Air Force Colonel Goldwater demonstrated his devotion to the principle that all men are equal before the law when he desegregated the Air National Guard. City Councilman Goldwater again demonstrated his concern when he moved to prevent segregation at the Phoenix Municipal Airport.

Private citizen Goldwater has, on many occasions, committed his energies to the service of the less fortunate. In the late forties, northern Mexico suffered a disastrous flood. Meager sanitary facilities, too few doctors and scanty medical supplies were inadequate to cope with the threatened epidemic of disease.

Goldwater organized and flew relief missions carrying medical supplies and food to those areas of the state of Sonora, isolated by the flood waters.

Bill Lester, radio reporter and program manager of station KOY, covered the relief operation. Many years later he provided this intimate glimpse of Goldwater through the eyes of an impartial observer.

"The pilot looked so haggard as he unfolded his big, lanky frame from the small plane, I didn't even want to approach him with my microphone. But the boss said, 'Get an interview' . . . so I tried. The mechanic nearby had just told me how many flights this pilot had made without stopping, so I tried the soft approach. 'Hi,' I said, 'I know you're awfully tired, but could you talk with the folks on radio for just a minute or two?' His face changed quickly from the haggard, hollow-eyed look to a friendly grin.

" 'Sure,' he answered, 'fire away.'

"So I asked about his flights, one right after another over the flooded areas of Mexico. Did the stranded Mexicans get the food and clothing? Were the flood waters going down yet? How many more trips did he have to make? How come he had to keep flying one volunteer flight after another? How long since his face had felt a razor? Didn't his coordination suffer after so many hours in the air? And he had a cheerful answer for everything I fired in his direction . . . tired . . . worn-out . . . haggard . . . unshaven . . . with clothes so mussed and wrinkled and dirty that the mechanic seemed spic 'n span by comparison. Yet, he gave me a smile, and the interview, and then excused himself to fly more supplies to the people he didn't know. They needed his help, and he couldn't rest until he gave all he could. I've interviewed Barry Goldwater many times since that visit to Sky Harbor Airport some 15 years ago: in his business office in Phoenix, as a member of the City Commission, as a campaigner and United States Senator, but I feel I met the real Barry the day I met the tired, eye-strained young pilot who took time to smile and hurry to serve where he could."

In many ways the 1952 campaign was a wonderful reflection of the personality of the candidate: simple, uncomplicated, uncluttered by elaborate campaign organization and extensive staff. Mel Harris, Barry's long-time personal secretary, kept the campaign schedule. Hoyt Pinaire, gifted comptroller for the Goldwater stores, kept track of expenditures, and strategy was decided in campaign headquarters where we had one secretary, a telephone and two typewriters.

The regular Republican Party organization, which had undergone a real blood-transfusion as a result of the Pyle victory, was in many ways a personal Goldwater organization. Pyle was running for re-election, and the regulars, smelling victory, gave their all.

The population of Arizona is concentrated in the urban areas centered around Tucson and Phoenix. The two counties, Maricopa, where Phoenix is located, and Pima, the county surrounding Tucson, account for about seventy-five percent of the population. Tucson, with a long established history as a permanent place of habitation, is quite naturally resentful of the greater growth in the upstate farm area around Phoenix.

The City of Phoenix had its genesis in the organization of the irrigation project from the waters of the Salt River in the year 1867. The Jesuit missionaries, and later the Franciscans, developed and directed civilized communities in the southern half of the state commencing in 1690. The old pueblo, Tucson, had been a Spanish city at least one hundred years before the first farmer thought about agriculture in central Arizona.

Every one familiar with the antagonisms between Los Angeles and San Francisco, California, can easily recognize the kind of silly pride which operates to split Arizona politically and economically. This split requires a candidate whose residence is in Maricopa County to devote a great deal of effort to the Pima County voters. In the spring of 1952, about the time Barry announced he would become a candidate for the United States Senate, a fairly prominent and presentable Pima County Republican announced his candidacy for the Senate.

The Republican Party was going to have a primary contest. Old-timers scratched their heads and tried to remember when this had happened before. If the party divided on geographical lines, Barry could expect to win, but the wounds of a primary are frequently fatal by the time general election day rolls around.

Barry told his friends that unless he could triumph over his Republican opponent in Pima County, the chances for victory in the fall would be slim indeed.

In addition to his liability as a Maricopa man, Goldwater also suffered from the fact that he had been a member of the Phoenix City Council, and while the rivalry between the counties is always evident, the warfare between the cities is bitter and unrelenting.

During the primary Barry spent most of his days in Tucson. He never once mentioned his opponent by name; he grinned when others mentioned the opposition to him. In this situation his long-established ties with the University of Arizona, which is located in Tucson and is the focal point of local pride, began to operate in Barry's behalf. Pima County residents were not content just to say, "Yes, I know Barry." They reacted to his candidacy vigorously and effectively. This partisan reaction is in itself a reflection of the Goldwater personality. Strong and positive in his beliefs, loyal and ardent with his friends, Barry makes it very difficult for people to ignore him. It is true his enemies react in the same energetic fashion. Before primary election day rolled around,

there were very few neutrals. Goldwater defeated his opponent by 30,163 votes; but, while Barry was rolling up a total
primary support of 33,460, McFarland was endorsed by 108,-
992 Democratic voters.

When the general election campaign opened in September,
the former partners, Pyle and Goldwater, decided against
campaigning together.

"Every vote you get, Howard, is at least a half vote for
me," Barry said, "and vice versa. Separately we can visit with
twice as many people."

Pyle had been a good Governor; he had pursued an almost
nonpartisan policy in making appointments to state boards
and commissions. It is traditional to give an Arizona Governor a second term and Eisenhower was running for President.*

Late in October, 1952, McFarland advisers began to sense
the possibility that this race would not be the pushover they
had anticipated. Their candidate had made no attempt to
answer the Goldwater attack, pitching his entire campaign
on the hand-shaking, personal contact which had served so
well in 1940 and 1946.

---

\* Long before the Republican delegation went to the 1952 National Convention, Goldwater had taken up the cudgels in behalf of his wartime commander. At the State Republican Convention, which was extremely pro-Taft
in sentiment, Goldwater had argued against an instructed delegation. Barry
had great admiration for Taft. He believed that either candidate would put
a halt to the welfare state policies of the Roosevelt-Truman era, and while
he privately believed Taft would receive the nomination, he was opposed to
closing the door to other contenders.

Barry still believes that delegates to a national convention should be free
to use their own best judgment in the selection of a candidate. This conviction, that cut-and-dried conventions, assembled to rubber-stamp decisions
reached as the result of political manipulations completed months and sometimes years in advance are harmful to the Republic, was responsible for
Barry's decision not to silence those supporters who were so insistent that
his name be presented to the 1960 National Convention.

In a last minute attempt to stem the tide they sensed was turning against them, McFarland's strategists published a full-page, black-type newspaper ad attacking Barry's war record. The ad suggested that because Barry owned a summer home in La Jolla, California, he should be regarded as a citizen of that state. The newspaper blast was supported by a radio broadcast voiced by a fellow member of the Quiet Birdmen * whom Barry had long regarded as a friend.

Barry did own a home in La Jolla, California. He had built it because the doctors suspected that Peggy was suffering from a pulmonary disease and advised a less severe summer climate. Barry, who was alway busy with some project in Arizona, had never spent any great amount of time at that south coast resort city. But the ad was a clever appeal to greed and envy, and the McFarland people felt confident their assault, launched on the week end before the general election, would achieve the desired results.

Goldwater, who had time purchased on two statewide radio networks on election eve, plus thirty minutes on the state's only television station, was at first inclined to ignore this attempt as a last minute smear. Ultimately he acknowledged it with a response that was more of a question than defense. "I have never shown this man anything but kindness. How he could do what he did is beyond my understanding."

The people understood. They went to the polls on that Tuesday morning in November and gave Goldwater a plurality of almost seven thousand votes, and Arizona had its first Republican Senator since 1920.

---

* A nationwide organization of pioneer airplane pilots formed in the early twenties.

CHAPTER **XIV**

# FRESHMAN SENATOR

**I**F, as many people believe, Barry Goldwater is a child of destiny, support for this conclusion can be found in the significant events of his first term as a Senator.

No man ever walked down the aisle to be sworn in with greater respect for the responsibilities of his office than Barry Goldwater. He had two ambitions: to serve the best interest of the nation and the State of Arizona; and to earn and deserve the respect of his colleagues, in that order.

Barry was only three years old in 1912, when Carl Hayden was first elected to the Congress. Hayden's family was as firmly rooted in the pioneer beginnings of Arizona as was Goldwater's. Barry's father had been a good friend and admirer of the Democratic Senator, and Barry, who doesn't stand in awe of many men, regards Hayden with affectionate respect. Standing in the United States Senate with this venerable public figure as his sponsor was an experience Barry will cherish until the day of his death.

Although a Democrat, Hayden was genuinely sincere in welcoming Barry to Washington. He was helpful in the many ways an old hand could be helpful, and when Barry asked Carl for advice, Hayden promptly told him the way to be a success was to vote with your party and keep your mouth shut for at least the first four years of your term.

During his almost fifty years of service in the Congress, Carl Hayden has followed his own advice. He rarely makes a speech on the Senate floor, is extremely shy and aloof with the press, and devotes most of his energies to fulfilling his committee assignments.

It has worked well for Carl Hayden. It has won him re-election twelve times. His seniority secured for him the coveted chairmanship of the Appropriations Committee, and when the Democrats reorganized the Senate in 1954, Carl Hayden was named President *pro tem.*

Barry thanked the Senator for his words of wisdom. They might do very well for Carl Hayden. In fact, they had done well for him; but it was totally impossible for Goldwater to follow such a course.

Because Arizona is a reclamation state, Barry fondly hoped for assignment to the Interior Committee. But there were others with greater seniority who also wanted Interior, and Majority Leader Taft was unable to grant Goldwater his preference. The other committee assignment which held particular interest for Barry was Military Affairs. Following his release from active duty in 1945, he had initiated, sponsored, and been the first commander of an Air National Guard Unit in Arizona.* He had not permitted anything to interfere with

---

* Barry insisted the outfit be created as an integrated unit. Arizona's Adjutant General reluctantly agreed, at the same time stating his opposition to integration of the Infantry forces. While on the City Council, Goldwater and his friend, Harry Rosenzweig, wrote into the lease for the Sky Chef's Dining Room at Municipal Airport an anti-segregation clause.

the continuation of his military career; and, since going to the Senate, he has completed the necessary academic courses in reserve training to earn promotion to the rank of Brigadier General.

But the Military Affairs Committee was likewise a desired spot. Once again the Majority Leader informed the freshman Senator from Arizona there was no room. When Bob Taft asked him to accept an assignment on the Labor Committee, Barry was completely mystified. Arizona in that year had very little industry; union organization was centered in the building trades, and Barry had never had any experience with compulsory unionism as practiced by the CIO and the UAW. He felt he was being pigeon-holed and put into a spot where his only function was to warm a chair.

Senator Taft argued that, as a business man completely free of any prejudice, Barry could make a useful contribution. Goldwater had never read the full text of the voluminous Taft-Hartley Act. He shared the opinion, prevalent in most non-industrial states, that this legislation had ended union abuse. However, there was little to be gained by protest, and Barry reluctantly accepted Taft's decision.

It was this assignment he didn't want, this committee berth he had never considered, which ultimately led to his service on the McClellan Select Committee to investigate labor and management.

Vice President Nixon has said many times, "Success in politics is conditioned on being in the right place at the right time." Goldwater's star was favorable on the day he acquiesced to Taft's suggestion. Originally the investigation into the practices of union labor was to have been conducted by the permanent Senate Committee on Investigations. On second thought it appeared likely that some legislative suggestions might come out of the hearings, and therefore it would be desirable to include members of the committee which, under Senate practices, would initiate labor legislation.

The leadership compromised and selected four members from the permanent Committee on Investigations and four from the Senate Labor Committee. Goldwater, being the second ranking member of Labor, was automatically included.

Barry's violent and vocal disagreement with Walter Reuther was inevitable; and the union bosses, in their attempt to destroy Goldwater, are primarily responsible for making his name a household word.

In the early months of 1953, as a new and inexperienced member of the Labor Committee, Barry busied himself acquiring a background of information. He was amazed to discover that many practices, unjust to the individual union members, were still permitted under the Taft-Hartley Act. Mike Bernstein, a brilliant and talented lawyer who had been assigned to the committee by Bob Taft, was Barry's instructor. Bernstein and Ray Hurley, another staff member, supplied Goldwater with case histories and specific instances of monopolistic union tactics.

In his first session, Barry introduced an amendment to the Taft-Hartley Act, which would have transferred to the several states the right to control and regulate strikes, picketing, lockouts and secondary boycotts.

"My amendment wasn't adopted," Barry says now, somewhat ruefully, "but it did accomplish one thing. It stopped all other proposed legislation in the labor field. The opposition, thinking I had enough votes to pass the amendment, moved quickly to recommit. The upshot of the whole thing was to end all proposed Taft-Hartley changes."

Barry's first full-fledged debate in the Senate was with George of Georgia over an aspect of foreign aid. Barry believes it is useless to buy friends. He also thinks there should be some *quid pro quo* for taxpayer dollars sent overseas in the Christmas baskets marked "foreign aid."

"I introduced an amendment to disallow France four hundred million in foreign aid unless she would offer some semblance of self-determination to her colonies in Southeast Asia.

"Senator George opposed me. Said it was wrong to tie strings to a gift and all that sort of thing. Then he promised the Senate that this was going to be the last foreign aid bill George of Georgia would approve.

"I lost my amendment and George voted for foreign aid as long as he remained in the Senate."

Goldwater was a good pupil and the masters of the Senate were stern teachers. For all the courtly language and outward display of courtesy, the ritual of initiation leaves its mark on the pledges.

In 1961, when the Kennedy Administration's lavish proposals for federal aid-to-education appeared to have sufficient votes for passage, Goldwater remembered the history of his first labor amendment.

"I couldn't beat them," he says with a grin, "so I offered to join them. I said, 'let's open the grab bag to everybody,' and proposed an amendment which would provide loans to private and parochial schools. No one wanted to be on record with a vote in opposition to the Roman Catholic Church and its educational program. The private schools have their friends, too. There was only one way out, and they took it. They voted to table the whole thing."

When his first year in the Senate ended, and the expenses were totaled, Barry was shocked. "When I used to hear politicians talk about their great sacrifice, I thought they were just bidding for sympathy," Barry says. "But I found out what they were talking about. The Senatorial allowance for travel doesn't begin to cover the demands, and every Senator is out-of-pocket. If you don't go home every time there is an opportunity, the people may not send you back when it comes time for re-election. If you do go home, and you live west of the Mississippi River, it's bound to cost you two or three thousand dollars a year."

When Barry was making his first campaign, he called on a newspaper editor in Wickenburg, Arizona. The editor angrily displayed a piece of franked mail he had received that day from one of Arizona's Senators. "Look at this," he demanded. "It's campaign material, pure and simple; and this fellow, who represents me in the Senate, used my money to send out his publicity."

Barry, who was running against the offending Senator, made a vow never to use the franking privilege on any piece of mail which was not strictly required by his Senatorial duties. Postage for his personal letters to constituents, not devoted entirely to official business, costs Barry about fifteen hundred dollars a year.

Like most freshman Senators, Barry began his career determined to employ only bona fide Arizona residents in his Senate office. He selected Mrs. Henry Coerver to be chief of his secretarial staff. Quick-witted, capable Edna smooths and sometimes completely smothers the many vexing problems which occur each day.

Henry Zipf, a big affable lawyer from Tucson, was Barry's first administrative assistant. Hank, who left the Senator's office in 1954 to make an unsuccessful bid for Congress from Arizona's Second District, was replaced by Charles Farrington.

In March of 1955, Dean Burch, a sharp, aggressive, law graduate from the University of Arizona, became Barry's special legislative assistant. More than a year before the 1958 campaign started, Burch succeeded Farrington.

"Dean was a great help to me all through the McClellan Committee hearings," Barry says. "We became close personal friends. I could always count on Dean when the going was really rough."

Barry goes out of his way to express appreciation for the staff members. They, in turn, respond with a warm loyalty. Pretty Elva Wingfield, who came to the Senator's office shortly after leaving high school, dislikes living in Washington but prefers working long hours for the Senator to any of the good jobs she might have in Arizona.

There have been staff changes over the years, and Barry has discovered that it isn't always possible to fill his requirements with Arizonans willing to live in Washington. Jan Smith, Mary Reynolds and Judy Rooney, whom he calls his supply sergeants, are as partisan Goldwater fans as any native Arizonan.

Dean Burch left after the 1958 election to practice law in Tucson; and his spot was taken by Ted Kazy, an extremely capable newspaper man, formerly employed on the *Arizona Republic*. Recently Tony Smith, a Washington newsman with considerable Capitol Hill experience, was brought in to help Ted with the increased work load, which is a reflection of Barry's growing national prominence.

Goldwater critics have attempted to exaggerate the times Barry has opposed programs of the Eisenhower Administration. They would like to picture Goldwater as being against everything, but the Senator's voting record gives a different picture.

"I have opposed the Administration at times," Barry says. "As long as I am here, and capable of thinking for myself, I'll probably never agree one hundred percent with the rest of the Republicans. But most of the time I voted with Ike, and when I had to vote against him," he says with a grin, "it was because I believe the staff and some members of the cabinet had persuaded the boss to go against his own better judgment."

As an example of this, Barry recalls that he and Eisenhower traveled across country in an airplane one time. Some of the states were suffering from a drought, and Ike expressed his satisfaction over the fact they were meeting their local problems.

"Ten days later we had an Administration bill calling for, as I remember it, seventy-five million dollars in federal drought aid. I was against it; I don't know what changed Ike's mind."

Barry had great respect for the members of Ike's cabinet as individuals and administrators. He didn't rate their political acumen too highly.

"Art Summerfield and Fred Seaton were the only two with much political experience," he says. "If we had cleaned out the policy-making civil servants who were carryovers from the Truman administration, most of our troubles never would have happened.

"We started to do this, but somewhere the signals were switched; and so, for eight years, much of the policy-making of real government was performed by holdover Democrats. It's no wonder the ideas the Eisenhower Administration cranked into the top came out upside down."

The investigations of the McClellan Committee monopolized Barry's interest in '57 and '58. He received more than fifteen thousand letters from union members, protesting against various evil and unjust practices of union bosses. Dozens of rank and file members came to Washington at their own expense to report their personal experiences to the Senator.

"You might think from reading the testimony of the hearings," Goldwater says, "that all labor unions are bad and all union bosses evil. Unfortunately, much of the testimony we heard would give this impression. On the whole, the union movement has been good for the country; and most union leaders are solid, decent citizens, making a substantial contribution to their home communities. The few rotten eggs created a stench, and that is what the public smells."

Goldwater's opposition to the activities of the UAW was generated by that union's history of monopolistic practices and by Walter Reuther's extravagant expenditure of union funds for political purposes.* Barry recognizes the red-headed union boss' ability, adroitness and dedication; and this, so far as Barry is concerned, strengthens the possibility that Reuther may achieve his goal of socialism through political means. Goldwater's belief that Reuther is dedicated to socializing the nation led him, in an unguarded moment, to describe Reuther as a greater menace than the Communist threat.

---

* $725,000 spent by the UAW-CIO in support of Senator McNamara in Michigan in 1954. (Hon. Ralph W. Gwinn of N.Y. in the U.S. House of Representatives, Monday, March 24, 1958.)

Reuther responded to Goldwater's criticism by suggesting the Arizona Senator needed psychiatric care.

If a man is to be judged by the complexion and power of his enemies, as well as by the quality of his friends, Barry's first term in the Senate would demand recognition for the notable enemies he earned.

CHAPTER **XV**

# THE 1958 CAMPAIGN—
# FIGHTING FOR SURVIVAL

HIS smashing re-election victory in 1958 blasted the widely held belief that 1952 had been a freak. Senator Barry Goldwater was thrust into the national political limelight. Professional politicians, who posture before the public wearing their togas of aloof superiority, proclaim devotion to sweet reasoned objectivity. They nod their heads in agreement with the Olympian logic emanating from such repositories of wisdom as *The New York Times*. They profess deep personal affection for their brothers in arms regardless of party affiliation. They rationalize every action, pontificate at the drop of a question, evade and avoid their constituents' queries, but they read the results of the ballot box loud and clear.

From 1952 to 1958 Goldwater was regarded as a charming, personable young fellow, whose strongly-voiced convictions added interest and, on occasion, embarrassment to the work of the world's greatest deliberative body. His forth-right approach to the problems of national concern was frequently disconcerting. His fellow members tolerated him and sometimes displayed affection for this lean Westerner, whose blunt, uncomplicated logic was as clear and consistent as the blue skies of his native state. But no one in Washington, Republican or Democrat, cherished any illusions that such a man could be re-elected from such a state as Arizona.

The Congress remained in session long after its usual date for adjournment in 1958, and when the weary members finally closed the books on the 85th Session, one and all, from pages to party leaders said, "Goodbye, Goldwater."

The campaign itself developed into all that is good and bad in the American political system. Supporters whose devotion reached hysterical peaks pounded the pavement with armloads of Goldwater literature, begging their neighbors to become acquainted with the virtues of this man who enlisted their most fanatical allegiance. There were anonymous smear sheets, fake telephone calls, threats of death to the Senator, his family and many connected with his campaign. There was an attempt to sabotage his airplane. At the last moment a particular effort to discredit Barry very nearly succeeded.

Ernest McFarland, who had never accepted the reality of his defeat in 1952, became the Democratic candidate for Governor in 1954 and won a close contest, triumphing over Howard Pyle who was then seeking his third term.

As Governor, McFarland skillfully used all the resources of patronage and administration to build a personal political following. To his intimates it was apparent Mac had little interest in the governorship; his heart was set on returning to the Senate, and more particularly on meeting Goldwater again.

As time for the 1956 elections drew near, the McFarland machine, according to a number of competent observers, carefully appraised the chance their hero had of winning the Democratic Senate seat held by Carl Hayden. Such an effort they recognized as a risky gamble. Hayden was popular and, despite his almost eighty years, still quite vigorous and fully capable of waging an energetic primary campaign. McFarland forces discreetly voiced a vain hope that maybe Uncle Carl would retire and leave the door open for his younger former colleague.

Throughout that spring of 1956, the McFarlandites carefully took the temperature of Arizona's political climate; when the time came for public declarations, McFarland announced for Governor, allowing the Senior Senator to claim the Democratic nomination unopposed.

In 1956 the voters of Arizona once again demonstrated their independence. They gave the state's electoral vote to Eisenhower, re-elected McFarland Governor by a whopping 55,000 majority, and sent Carl Hayden back to the Senate to begin his forty-fifth year of service in the United States Congress.

Hayden's Republican opponent in the general election, a well-qualified lawyer named Ross Jones, had served two terms as Attorney General. Jones, with full approval of Republican Party leaders, waged a token campaign. There was no real effort made to defeat Hayden. When the '56 campaign plans were being formulated, Barry informed his party that if this was to be a serious effort, he would stump the state for Jones.

"You know I have a great personal admiration for Carl

Hayden," he said, "but Hayden is a Democrat and we need a Republican. The decision is up to you."

The party leaders recognized that, even with Eisenhower seeking re-election, the odds were against Hayden's defeat. Moreover, there was a real danger that if too much vigor were displayed in the Senate race, the voters might evidence their displeasure by going against Eisenhower.

Such practical decisions may offend the unrealistic idealists, but they are made every day. The Presidency was considered of greater importance than the Senate seat. Barry, whatever his enemies might say about him, has always demonstrated party loyalty and accepted the judgment of the state Republican leadership.

The 1958 campaign was a repeat, in many ways, of the 1952 situation. This time Goldwater was the incumbent, McFarland the challenger—and the odds were reversed: the challenger was picked to win.

The McFarland Administration may not have made any notable contributions during its four years in office, but it certainly made no political mistakes. The swords were freshly ground, the spears had been retipped, and the cross bowmen were in position ready to advance.

Every local prognosticator with any claim to fame, and the full complement of outside observers who flashed through Arizona to feel the grass roots, sided with McFarland. *Time Magazine;* Marquis Childs; Gladwin Hill, the erudite correspondent of *The New York Times;* and a host of others were able to see only one possible outcome. Many of Goldwater's staunch Republican supporters expressed serious misgivings.

Political campaigns are a combination of many elements. They are operated in an almost carnival atmosphere; everyone involved becomes a matchless expert: *you're not doing enough—you're doing too much—the candidate should say this—the candidate mustn't say that—for heaven's sake avoid this issue—for goodness sake come out four-square on this issue—where are the billboards?—the other fellow's got all the television time—your messages are not getting home— what have you done, given up?* The one voice of reasoned sanity in that entire hectic, frustrating and sometimes frightening period belonged to the candidate himself. Barry never wavered; he never showed any disposition to depart from the strategy which had been established. He accepted the failure of supporting technical services as though it were par for the course.

Timing is always important in any effort to enlist the unified action of a great, diverse group of individuals. When the timing of the 1958 campaign was established early in 1957, prominent Republicans pleaded with Barry to alter his strategy. When this failed, they shouted at him, and when they still didn't get results, they sulked. Invariably Barry's reply was the same, "Well, suppose you talk to Steve, but I think we're doing it right."

Candidates for public office frequently make the fatal mistake of believing it is necessary to reach and convince a majority of the electorate in order to be victorious. Consequently, they put together a grab bag collection of appeals, promises and arguments calculated to motivate every segment of the population.

Frequently, such scattergun tactics result in defeat and leave the candidate completely mystified over the reasons for his failure.

In any election, even in Arizona where the registration odds heavily favor the Democrats, the general election candidate who has gone through the primary, or has been unopposed for nomination, can count on the unwavering support of a certain percentage of the total of those qualified to vote. If the candidates and party have habitually received forty percent of the total of the vote cast, it can be assumed that any reasonable candidate of that party enters the contest with a solid forty percent support. If this premise be true, eleven percent of the electorate becomes the magic number, because eleven percent added to the solid forty can mean victory.

Many people have little or no interest in elections until the final weeks of the campaign. Lacking any strong political convictions, they postpone making their decision—indeed many do not decide until the actual election day. These are the people who must be reached and motivated to support a candidate if victory is to be the outcome.

Partisan party members have their minds made up long before the candidates are selected. In a traditional one-party state such as Arizona, it can be anticipated that perhaps forty or forty-five percent of the registered voters are unlikely to vote against their party candidate.

All of the national public opinion polls tend to support this theory. At the beginning of a contest it is never possible to find a majority who will express their opinion in favor of one particular candidate. Sometimes the pollsters adopt the expedient of using the category which they describe as "leaning toward" one candidate or the other. It might be argued that this swing or switch vote, comprised largely of individuals who have no strong political convictions, is actually a menace to popular government. Their vote invariably decides an election outcome, and thus we have the paradox of those who are least interested being responsible for the ultimate decision.

If this concept of election contests is valid, it follows that the deciding segment of the electorate, individuals who have only a minor interest in government, must be approached with a positive and readily grasped appeal. The voter who is still undecided two weeks before election day obviously lacks the background or interest to decide between the varying shades of grey which frequently separate candidates. To reach this group, it is necessary to emphasize those principles and aspects which constitute a major or striking difference between the two contenders. It is also advisable to present the candidate's views in terms of the voter's genuine interest. If the major concern of the community is Deepwater Seaborn Transport, the candidate who speaks of Outer Space is asking for defeat.

Early in 1957, we commenced on behalf of Barry's candidacy to conduct a series of completely unscientific public opinion samplings. What we hoped to determine, if possible, was the major concern of the majority of citizens in each Arizona community. The procedures followed would, I'm sure, be regarded as absurdly inadequate by any of the professionals in the sampling field, but they did produce what we accepted as a reliable consensus of informed public concern. Before the campaign was over our returns were validated over and over again.

The major differences between the candidates were obvious even to the disinterested, unaffected observer. Barry put all his cards on top of the table; he was blunt and unequivocal; he was young and vigorous, and after six years of seasoning he had become a skillful public speaker whose straight-forward messages glistened with sincerity and purpose.

McFarland was still a courthouse politician. Never a forceful orator, his unwillingness to take a clear-cut stand on any question gave his audiences an impression of halting indecision. Mac's great political asset was his ability to shake hands with people, and a kind of tireless determination which kept him everlastingly at it.

Goldwater's part in the probings of the McClellan Committee had earned the determined animosity of Walter Reuther and most of the big labor union bosses. In their Miami Convention, held in the spring of '58, organized labor listed as its number one political objective the defeat of the Junior Senator from Arizona.

McFarland had the friendly support of organized labor, but this labor assistance had cost him dearly in local reputation.

When the McClellan Committee was questioning Brewster of the Teamsters Union, it was developed that this body had contributed $4,000 in the form of a check to McFarland's 1956 campaign for governor.* The money had not been reported, a clear violation of Arizona's election law. McFarland had first placed the blame for failure to comply with the statutory requirements on Joseph C. Duke, then Sergeant-at-Arms of the United States Senate, an Arizona Democrat with a host of friends.

Duke, who is frequently called upon to assist Democratic Senators in their election campaigns, was a McFarland partisan and because of his keen political insight and wide personal acquaintance, had been able to contribute materially to McFarland's defeat of Pyle in 1954. Joe Duke had been a campaign adviser to McFarland in 1956, but he had not handled the finances, and when Mac attempted to blame him

---

* Page 45 of the hearings, McClellan Select Committee.

by saying he turned the Teamsters' check over to Duke, the charge was promptly repudiated.

Mac then remembered the check had been transferred to an advertising man who had used the proceeds for normal campaign expenditures.

The failure to report might have been nothing more than an innocent oversight, not at all unusual in the pressure of political warfare. But the unpleasant memory of Mac's vain attempt to evade responsibility alienated a number of knowledgeable supporters who would otherwise have been in his corner—experienced campaigners who might have prevented some of the costly McFarland mistakes in 1958.

Aside from the problems of timing which are almost entirely technical, Barry viewed 1958 as a challenge in three parts. Union bosses throughout the country were committed to go all out in their efforts to use union political strength. Consequently, it was necessary that Barry make a direct appeal to the men who worked with the tools, to separate them, if possible, from the stewards and the union hierarchy.

It was also necessary to reach the thinking Democrat capable of independent action. There is an old phrase developed in the East to describe partisan followers who are incapable of voting for anyone other than the party candidate—they are known variously as "yellow dog Republicans" and "yellow dog Democrats," the explanation being they would vote for a yellow dog if a yellow dog were bearing the party label. Goldwater realized it was necessary to separate the nominal Democrats from those who would vote for any candidate bearing the Democratic party label.

The third challenge, and perhaps first in importance, was to motivate every registered Republican and then to

establish machinery to insure that every Republican got to
the polls and voted.

Once again the formal campaign was opened in Prescott
early in September. From the opening gun to midnight the
day before the general election, the campaign was a display
of techniques which thrilled and chilled the voters. Sweet
reason was trampled underfoot. It was a bare-knuckle contest with no holds barred, like the fight of two backwoods-
men eye-gouging, kneeing, scratching and biting. More than
political victory or political defeat was at stake. Both men
were fighting for survival as public figures. One could survive. There is no agony comparable to the death of a public
career—and death was in store for the loser.

# CHAPTER XVI

# SMEAR, SLANDER, SABOTAGE
# AND VICTORY

ERNEST MCFARLAND approached 1958 with none of
the over-confidence which had, perhaps, cost him victory in
1952. He had a dozen or more campaign specialists, especially recruited because of their acknowledged skill in one
or more phases of campaigning.

A number of Republicans, and a good many conservative
Democrats, had been disappointed by the failure of the
Eisenhower administration to halt the growth of bureaucracy
in Washington and reduce public expenditure. The people
of Arizona still liked Ike, but they made no attempt to conceal their lack of enthusiasm for some of the men on Ike's
team. The Sherman Adams scandal had given effective
ammunition to the Democrats. It was difficult for Republicans to convince the voters that all of the failures of the
Eisenhower administration should be placed at the door of a

Democrat-controlled House and Senate. The political winds
had reversed. The Republicans, who had been on the attack
in 1952, were now on the defensive.

In the first quarter of 1958 the nation suffered from a
rather sharp economic recession. Severe unemployment and
an alarming slump in sales added grist to the mills of Democratic publicists.

Two serious errors were committed by the Goldwater
forces in September, 1958. One Barry still regrets, the other
he now believes developed into an asset rather than a liability.

In his opening speech at Prescott, when Barry reviewed
the Senate record of McFarland, he credited his opponent
with having voted "no" on an issue of some significance to
the people of the state.

McFarland's press experts demanded an immediate apology and offered proof that their ex-Senator had, in fact,
voted "yes" on the issue.

The basis for Goldwater's charge was a memo on the voting record of Senator McFarland supplied by the Republican
staff in Washington. Unfortunately the researchers had done
a sloppy job. The actual vote had been "no", but, as in so
many legislative decisions, a "no" vote on this particular bill
was, in fact, a "yes" vote supporting the important principle.

It was a serious mistake, one which might affect the outcome of the election. However, Barry decided that McFarland had made his point. Any public apology or public
recognition of the error on the part of Goldwater would only
serve to keep the issue alive in the newspapers and on radio
and television.

"I'm not going down this blind alley with Mac," Barry
said. "We goofed, he knows it, he's made our fault public,

but how he voted in 1950 is not the primary issue between us."

This decision was a testimony to the political wisdom Goldwater had acquired during his six years of service in the Senate. Dozens of elections have been lost when a candidate allows himself to be diverted from the principal issue. Skillful campaign managers deliberately create these side-alley disputes. If a candidate can be persuaded to engage in an argument over something not truly germane, public attention is led to consideration of the unimportant while the significant issue is ignored.

In the 1952 Presidential campaign there was a very real attempt to make the Nixon-Stevenson funds major issues. Whether or not the newly-elected President would go to Korea had very little to do with the differences in political philosophy offered by candidates Stevenson and Eisenhower. Yet Ike's dramatic statement, which was in many ways a side-alley diversion, certainly had a tremendous bearing on his election.

After four or five days of complaining about the Goldwater error, McFarland discovered he had no one to complain to, and the matter was soon forgotten.

The second error might have been far more serious. Political television commercials, presented as twenty-, thirty-, and sixty-second station-break segments, are generally agreed to be an effective means of reaching the politically indifferent voter.

Because of the long session of the Congress, Barry's initial television announcements were made hurriedly under somewhat adverse conditions. The camera work left much to be desired, and the whole effect smacked of amateur enthusiasm. The McFarland commercials, on the other hand, had been done with the assistance of experts. Mac had gone to California to utilize the best technical people in the field. His films were beautifully put together. The photography was excellent, and the script concise and compelling.

The reaction from Goldwater supporters was a loud wail of anguish. To them it seemed their candidate had been outgunned and destroyed by the slick McFarland TV clips.

Far more successfully than anything that might have been achieved by a planned appeal, these poorly made television spots aroused Barry's friends; they felt compelled to do something effective personally to make up the lost ground. Ultimately it was the dedicated political activity of hundreds of people all over the state which produced the remarkable and satisfying results.

There was a second factor in this TV interchange which has never been revealed. McFarland's copy was designed to make him appear as the father of all irrigation and reclamation projects in the state. Certainly his script writers can be excused for believing they were aiming their appeal at a receptive target. Arizona is a reclamation state. Prior to 1950 there was very little industry, and the entire economy was dependent upon irrigated agriculture. Their spots made Mac the father of all water; water is life in this barren state; therefore, Mac was a great benefactor.

Had the McFarland group been correct in its assumption, the outcome of that election might very well have been different, but the majority of the people in Arizona had no active interest in reclamation. At Goldwater headquarters we knew this. The unscientific samplings of public opinion, which were begun in 1957 and continued throughout the campaign, indicated that the progress of reclamation was of no concern to the majority of voters.

The surveys had been conducted by offering five or six subjects and asking those consulted to number the subjects in order of importance. Selection of the choice offered was usually dictated by current news emphasis, such as unemployment in the first quarter of 1958, the menace of Communism, the activities of the labor unions, federal fiscal policies, etc. Because reclamation is important to the economy of Arizona, we always included the current phase of reclamation development as one of the possible subjects.

In dozens of samplings the development of irrigation water was always in last place. McFarland had probably spent twenty-five thousand dollars on the TV spots, to talk about a subject which had no interest for his audience.

The campaign timetable was laid out in recognition of our belief that the voters who would actually decide the outcome—that is, those without firm political convictions—would probably not begin to make up their minds until three or four weeks before the first Tuesday in November. These people rarely attend political rallies, are not avid readers of newspaper accounts of campaign activities, and are, in many ways, the most difficult of all to reach and impress with the significance of a political contest.

In December of 1957 we contracted for what the outdoor advertising people call a one-hundred percent,* two-hundred percent * showing throughout the State of Arizona. About the time our billboards went on display, the McFarland camp began to scream that Goldwater was overspending, hoping to buy re-election. Their protest arose from the fact that when they tried to contract for billboard space all of the available boards had been rented. Since they couldn't

---

* An advertising term indicating the entire population will see the message. 200%—twice the exposure of the 100%.

match Goldwater's outdoor display, they tried to minimize its effectiveness by raising the old, hackneyed charge of lavish expenditure.

This had barely subsided when the McFarland people learned about the television arrangements for "simulcasts," and their safety valves popped wide open.

Beginning in May of 1958, Ivan Shun of Advertising Counselors, who was in charge of space and placement for the Goldwater campaign, started making arrangements to purchase the same half-hour segment on television on every channel in the state.* By linking the stations together it was thus possible to reach every television viewer who happened to be tuned in during that half-hour.

This tactic produced a great divergence of opinion in the Goldwater camp. Some maintained we would antagonize most of the viewers, who might wish to watch a favorite program. However, the "simulcasts" were scheduled: from nine to nine-thirty on election eve; nine to nine-thirty on the Thursday prior to election; and nine to nine-thirty on the Wednesday prior to the Thursday.

The objectives and aims were: (1) encouraging the active support of every Republican; (2) separating of reasonable Democrats from those who would blindly vote their party loyalty; and (3) reaching the men who worked with tools and separating them from the influence of union bosses. The actual TV presentations were designed to be as dramatic as possible. The most gifted orator in the world, standing immobile behind a podium, talking to a microphone and staring at a camera, would have difficulty holding an audience for thirty minutes.

---

* The simulcasts were Shun's idea. They proved to be the most effective advertising of the entire campaign.

The first television program presented less than ten minutes of Goldwater on camera. The rest of the time was devoted to clips from the filmed proceedings before the McClellan Select Committee. The angry testimony of Hoffa, Reuther, Brewster, Mazy and a host of others offered all the drama of a suspenseful, fictional TV program. The witnesses snarled at the committee, the Senators demanded answers and Goldwater commented on the proceedings.

The program was done before a live studio audience of some five hundred people who were present by invitation. Some of them had travelled more than three hundred miles to be there and support their candidate. The reaction of the live audience was tremendous, and there was an infectious spontaneity clearly reflected by the cameras as they cut from the cheering crowd to the smiling candidate.

The second program dealt specifically with Barry's proposals to provide the working union man with statutory protection: accountability for the spending of union dues; secret votes for strikes; the right of a union member to express his opinion without reprisal; the necessity for ending imposed trusteeships; and the grossly unfair "telephone booth" official meetings, where policy decisions are made contrary to the majority will of the members.

Following the second televised simulcast more than one hundred union members paid a visit to the Senator's headquarters in an outside county. They wanted Senator Goldwater to know that now, for the first time, they understood what he had been talking about.

The election-eve, final simulcast had been projected as a repetition of the 1952 climax, with Barry and his family in a pleasant, friendly atmosphere, but it didn't turn out that way. It was, by all odds, the most dramatic conclusion to any political campaign ever waged in the State of Arizona.

Following the CIO's public declaration of war on Goldwater, issued at the Miami meeting in the spring of 1958, rumors began to flow of unusual political union activity in Arizona.

How much was fact or how much was fiction we probably will never know, but there was sufficient supported truth in the rumors to warrant a careful investigation. Walter Reuther had named the defeat of Senator Barry Goldwater as his number one political objective. It was incumbent upon the Goldwater camp to learn how Reuther intended to proceed.

In early June a friendly trade-unionist reported unusual political activity in Tucson, where the western regional organizer for COPE had established headquarters in the Santa Rita hotel.

The union was screening potential candidates for the legislature, and, from some of those interviewed, it was learned that money and workers were promised to candidates the unions found acceptable.

The identity of the union political expert was quickly established, and when he moved to Phoenix and began contacting influential leaders in the McFarland group, we were promptly advised of his activity.

An enterprising newspaperman on the *Arizona Republic* asked the chairman of the Democratic Party in Arizona if his candidates were receiving labor union support; and, particularly, whether or not he had knowledge of any out-of-state labor political expert's activities.

The chairman categorically denied union support, and in a statement for publication said there were no outside political labor people interfering in the Arizona election. When the newspapers learned about the activity in Phoenix and

Tucson, they started a probe which produced some very damaging facts. The union organizer, whose name was Al Green, had a criminal record in California. He had been arrested in connection with some early acts of union violence. In Arizona he was in almost daily contact with the leaders of the Democratic Party. A photographer, seeking a scoop, got a good picture of Democratic state chairman Joe Walton, and the political expert, Al Green, leaving a downtown restaurant where they had lunched together.

The story was given front page coverage in most of the daily papers ten days before the general election. The carefully recruited and carefully trained union election-day teams, which had been established to work the precincts in Tucson and Phoenix, collapsed under the barrage of unfavorable publicity.

During the noon hour on Friday, October 31, 1958, an unidentified man distributed some handbills in the shopping areas of Phoenix. At 1:55 the first handbill was brought to Goldwater headquarters. It showed a line drawing of Joseph Stalin smoking his pipe and winking. The caption above the drawing was, "Why not vote for Goldwater." Below, there was a paste-up message implying that the United Mine, Mill and Smelter Workers Union and Goldwater would merit Stalin's support.

The whole presentation was preposterous. His enemies could accuse Goldwater of many things, but no one in his right mind would suggest that Barry was soft on communism. The Mine, Mill and Smelter Workers Union had purged itself of Communist sympathizers. Moreover, it had officially announced an endorsement for McFarland.

The pattern of distribution of the handbills was peculiar. They had been left in cars on East and West McDowell

Road; then three or four hundred had been placed in cars in the parking lot surrounding the Goldwater store.

The FBI was notified, but the local agent in charge could take no official action. As friends of Goldwater came to headquarters with copies of the handbill to express their indignation, some forty or fifty were accumulated. These were sent to the newspapers.

Such a flamboyant, nonsensical cartoon, distributed in the last minutes of a political campaign when emotions are frayed and tempers high, crowded all other public and political activity into the background.

By six o'clock Friday night, following a dozen reconstructions of the act, we concluded there must be a far more devious reason for the leaflet's distribution than was then in evidence.

McFarland was too skillful a campaigner to sponsor the distribution of a handbill which obviously was wide of its target; moreover, McFarland was acquainted with federal law and, had he been responsible, there would have been some evidence of authorship on the sheet. It was ridiculous to call Goldwater a Communist; therefore, the purpose of the handbill was not to call Goldwater a Communist, and there must be some other meaning.

Saturday morning the second act of the drama developed. A newspaper release from Washington announced that a staff employee of Senator Theodore Green's (Democrat-R.I.) Select Committee on Privileges and Elections, James H. Duffy, was en route to Arizona to investigate the distribution of an unsigned, smear handbill.

This indeed was quick action. An inquiry to the minority counsel of the Select Committee produced the amazing information that Duffy had made his plans to leave for Arizona on Thursday and had arranged his transportation twelve hours in advance of the appearance of the first handbill in Phoenix. We also learned that Roland Bibolet, McFarland's right-hand man, had made reservations for Duffy's hotel accommodations.

In the Goldwater headquarters we were puzzled. Was it possible that Duffy, and the other members of his committee, had possessed advance information on the leaflet? They had. In fact, some of the leaflets had been distributed in Yuma on Wednesday of that week. Apparently the matter had been brought to the Governor's attention, and his office had instituted the request for inquiry.

The political community buzzed with excitement. Duffy arrived, made a brief call on the newspaper which had printed the story of the pamphlet, telephoned the Senator's office, spoke with the publicity man, and did nothing more.

Sunday afternoon the Maricopa County Republican Chairman, Charles Garland, called and was greatly agitated. Agent Duffy had informed him of the existence of an affidavit claiming the cartoon pamphlet had originated in his office. When I relayed this information to Barry, he suggested that I try to find Duffy and determine what was going on.

The Senate Committee employee was in his room at the Sahara Motel, and he proved to be a pleasant, slightly-built man. He wouldn't show me the affidavit, but he gave me the name of the author. It was a name I recognized as belonging to a crackpot who, two weeks earlier, had been overheard by an off-duty Phoenix policeman threatening to kill Goldwater.

I had the policeman's statement in my office; Duffy went with me and took a copy when he left.

"I don't know where the cartoon was produced," I told him. "The County Chairman swears he doesn't know. I don't believe it would be wise to make a charge on the basis of the affidavit of a known crackpot."

Duffy agreed. He also agreed with my thinking that the cartoon was too stupid and pointless to be issued by the McFarland camp. I thought he believed me when I told him that, to my knowledge, no one in the Goldwater head-quarters had anything to do with the pamphlet or its distribution.

Monday morning the storm broke. Duffy released a state-ment to the newspapers in which he charged that the only widespread distribution of the pamphlet had been made by Stephen Shadegg, Goldwater's campaign manager. Then he checked out of his hotel room and disappeared.

Shortly after publication of the Duffy statement charging me with distributing the pamphlet, numerous McFarland supporters were on television, repeating the charge and attempting to create a belief that the Stalin pamphlet had been manufactured by the Goldwater campaigners with dia-bolical cunning, and had been distributed in order to smear McFarland by reverse inference.

A week after the votes were counted, I learned that the time for these special television charges had been contracted for on Friday, which seemed to indicate that McFarland's organization had anticipated Duffy's official statement.

The polls would open in just eighteen hours. We had fought a bitter, exhausting campaign. Barry had served his fellow citizens, and the nation, with great distinction for six years. Would all this now be swept away in a moment of last minute hysteria?

We knew the author of the pamphlet would be identified eventually, but by then it might be too late.*

This was the situation when Barry went before the television cameras at nine o'clock on that Monday election eve. He used ten minutes of the time introducing his family in a homey, quiet atmosphere which had been a part of our original plan. Then he turned his face to the camera and recited the events of the Stalin cartoon.

Why had Duffy purchased his tickets for the airline trip to Phoenix before anyone in Phoenix knew about the existence of the Stalin cartoon? What reasonable inquiry did Duffy make when he arrived in Phoenix? How could he accuse Stephen Shadegg of a widespread distribution of the cartoons when all Shadegg had done was to mail samples of the cartoon to some thirty newspaper editors throughout the state?

"Why didn't Duffy question me?" Goldwater demanded. "Why didn't he question Shadegg? Why didn't he question the people who found the handbill in the first place? And where is Duffy now? Nothing has been solved, no proof of responsibility has been produced.

"I'm here," Goldwater said to his audience. "Shadegg is here. Where is Duffy?"

It was a skyrocket finish to a campaign filled with emotion and danger.

In the very early stages there had been widespread dis-

---

* Frank Goldberg, 26, a Democrat and member of the International Association of Machinists, AFL-CIO, and Earl N. Anderson, 52, a one-time grand lodge representative for four Western states of the International Association of Machinists, were ultimately identified by the FBI as being responsible for the Stalin cartoon. Goldberg, at one time, was recording secretary of the machinists Local 763 at the Goodyear Corporation in Phoenix, and was a Democratic precinct committeeman. Both men were convicted in June, 1960.

semination of vicious, untrue stories assaulting Barry's marriage. These had been followed by equally untrue stories concerning working conditions in the Goldwater stores. An anonymous caller had telephoned threats of death to Mun; and dozens of strangers, many driving out-of-state cars, had been observed in political activity.

When it was first suggested that it would be prudent to place a guard around Barry's private airplane, most of us pooh-poohed the notion, and Barry flatly rejected the whole idea.

"If Walter Reuther wants to beat me," Goldwater said, "he doesn't fight that way." Fortunately we were all persuaded to change our minds. A man, long experienced in the political industrial warfare of the Midwest, made a trip to Phoenix to argue caution.

"Of course Reuther wouldn't order such a thing," he told us. "Jimmy Hoffa wouldn't either. No responsible union leader would even suggest the assassination of a United States Senator. But what about the fanatics? Some thug might be stupid enough to think he could make a career out of this thing. Airplanes are easy to sabotage. Just a little tinkering and we have one more unexplained accident in the air. No one is left to tell what happened."

Barry had leased a twin-engine Beech Bonanza for use in the campaign. He reluctantly approved arrangements to protect the aircraft. Two FBI-trained, former police officers, were hired to maintain a twenty-four-hour-a-day watch. Measured lengths of transparent cellophane tape were unobtrusively fixed to the doors and inspection ports of the aircraft. Control surfaces were carefully inspected before each flight, and in Phoenix the twin was kept in a private hangar, padlocked and secured in such a way as to reveal any unauthorized attempt to open the doors.

So far as we could determine, no one made any effort to tamper with the hangar or the airplane while it was in Phoenix. One sunny day when it was parked on a remote airstrip near Benson, all our precautions were justified.

The campaign party had arrived, and departed for town in two cars. The guard was inside the aircraft, where he could not be seen. A car containing four men approached, paused at the fence guarding the runway, and then cautiously crept forward.

The guard, who was expecting someone to return from town with sandwiches, straightened into view and stepped out on the wing. The car with its four occupants took off down the runway, finally turned off and blazed a trail across the desert, where there was no road.

It is possible the occupants of that car had no sinister purpose in mind when they attempted to approach the Goldwater airplane. If so, why the sudden flight? Why did they go down the runway when they might have turned around and used the normal exit? Was it because this course would have brought them close enough to the aircraft to be recognized?

The somewhat chagrined security guard provided a good description of the automobile, but he had been unable to see the license plates. By the time the campaign party returned from town, it was too late to take up pursuit. Had there been a telephone on the dirt strip the guard might have summoned help; had there been an automobile, he most certainly would have followed that fleeing car.

When Barry left the television studio on election eve, he went directly to the airport to fly to Yuma. Yuma was the one television outlet in the state he could not reach by cable; and since a kinescope would be too late, it had been arranged that Goldwater would fly to Yuma and repeat his broadcast live for viewers in that area.

Dean Burch, Barry's able and dedicated administrative assistant, who had helped discover the damaging information as to the circumstances of Duffy's trip to Arizona, suggested that since we knew Duffy had not left town, it might be worthwhile trying to find him.

We found him. At least we found out where he was by eleven o'clock that night. Duffy was with McFarland and Bibolet in the offices of television station KTVK, owned by the Governor.

Dean and I waited patiently for Duffy to return to his room in a resort hotel, a room which had been reserved for him by Roland Bibolet. When Duffy came in about one-thirty A.M. he was at first defiant and noncommittal; finally showing resentment over our questioning, he said, "Hell, Burch, you know what this is all about. You're a Republican, I'm a Democrat. I came out here to do a job and I did it."

The next day the voters of Arizona did their job. They gave Barry a 35,000 vote majority over McFarland.

CHAPTER **XVII**

## "THERE IS A TIDE IN
## THE AFFAIRS OF MEN"

No other form of human competition is comparable to a political contest. Winner take all does not begin to describe the fruits of victory. Crowds cheer the winner. The interests —money, business, labor, reclamation, conservation and a hundred more—fawn at the feet of the victor.

Caustic observers of the American political scene who complain about the corruption of public officials invariably suggest this is done by sliding money under the table. Actually, flattery is far more destructive. The candidate before election day is filled with doubts and misgivings, humble in his approach to subjects beyond his knowledge, eager for advice and willing to profit from criticism. But what a monstrous change takes place in the ego of most men when the official canvass declares the winner.

Some change is inevitable. When the candidate's convic-

tions—his expressed political philosophy—is vindicated and
approved by a majority of his constituents, there is bound
to be an increase in self-confidence. After all, this is part
of the purpose of elections—to permit the sovereign citizens
to accept or reject the total personality of the candidate.

When Barry returned to Washington in January 1959, he
quickly sensed the change in attitude toward him and his
conservative sentiments. This was particularly true of his
colleagues on the Democratic side of the aisle. Most of the
members of his own party were warmly pleased over his
re-election. The President went out of his way to let Barry
know he approved the action of the Arizona electorate.

Prior to 1958 Barry had received a pleasant, steady stream
of invitations to speak before conservative groups in various
sections of the country. In 1959 the stream became a deluge,
and they were not all from organizations and sponsors necessarily classified as conservative. The election results had
strengthened Goldwater's convictions regarding the validity
of his conservative philosophy. It also made him aware of
the deliberate misunderstanding fostered against the word
"conservative".* When liberal members of the press renewed
their attacks on him, he gloried in the fight. Here was no
stuffy octagenarian pleading for the retention of the *status
quo*. Goldwater is a prediction of tomorrow rather than a relic

---

* *Daytona Beach News Journal* editorial of May 7, 1961, questioned
whether Goldwater even believed in democracy. *The Arizona Labor Journal*,
Feb. 18, 1960, called Goldwater the party's "little fuhrer" and "golden boy."
Lyman H. Bookbinder, legislative representative AFL-CIO in Washington,
criticized Goldwater's statement that seven years of the New Deal did not
produce full employment—that not until our entry into World War II were
we able to provide jobs for all Americans. Bookbinder said: "Does not
Senator Goldwater realize that this is precisely the contention of the world
Communist movement? Does he really believe the Communist's line that the
American economic system needs war and preparation for war to avoid recession and unemployment?"

of yesterday, and his simple, earnest delineation of a forward-looking, progress-building philosophy of conservatism disarmed his critics and convinced many skeptics in his audiences.

In 1957, speaking to a Republican group in Arizona, Goldwater had said:

"I do not presume to speak for the Republican Party. I have no commission to express your political thinking. May I then crave your indulgence? May I enlist your most thoughtful consideration?

"Political institutions created by free men throughout our world are under constant assault, both abroad and at home. The wisdom of the past is being reviled and discarded.

"A thousand voices speak in confusion, offering tempting panaceas for each tortuous crisis. The voices of thoughtful men, speaking in disciplined debate, are shouted down by the hysterical name-callers.

"It may be that we are living at the end of an era: that our era ended in August of 1945, when the bomb dropped on Hiroshima; or that our era ended three weeks ago tomorrow night, when sputnik took up its orbit.

"To those voices of despair and prophets of doom may I proclaim, with all the sincerity at my command, that ideas and ideals are today, and always shall be, more powerful than aggression and material implements of aggression.

"The Republican Party, to which I pledge all my allegiance and my strength, serves the cause of freedom, seeking justice and equality for all men before the law.

"The Republican Party, to which I give my devotion, acknowledges with deep reverence the truths that Almighty God created men to be free and gave to his creation freedom of choice.

"The Republican Party I salute holds the concept that there was created on this continent a decentralized republic with a reprsentative form of government, dedicated to the concept of limited central authority, maximum individual opportunity, and equality and freedom for all men.

"May I now claim your attention while we, together, as American citizens of equal rights and equal voice and equal mutual responsibility, examine those specific areas where freedom is challenged and must be redeemed, if this nation under God is to endure.

"The enemy of freedom is compulsion, masquerading under a thousand false faces, cloaked frequently with the respectability of noble objectives. Compulsion is the Roman chariot of those self-professed, superior individuals, who regard you and me as incapable of solving our own problems, of meeting our own destinies.

"These self-appointed architects of our future would create a spoon-fed society—a society of neither height nor depth, but only breadth—by constant appeals to greed and envy, by exploiting the natural passions of minority groups, by force-feeding the flames of jealousy.

"These voices would divide and subjugate America to a listless common denominator, equal perhaps in material possessions and material activities and material accomplishments, but devoid of soul and spirit and freedom.

"I say these things are planned, are proposed, are objectives? Forgive me. These bitter, repugnant truths confront us today and are here in reality and must be faced. It is not pleasant to recognize the eroding-away of that which was the birthright of every American.

"In the past thirty bitter years the operations of the federal government have increased with geometrical proportions until today the compulsion of big government expresses its influence on the lives of every individual, until today the federal tax claims, before we receive it, more than thirty percent of all our labor.

"Compulsion in big labor extorts a tribute from every working man, and devotes the fruits of his muscles and brain to the service of causes and programs which are offensive to the very individual who is compelled to support them with money.

"The hands of big business are stained with past offenses—the employment of compulsion to create unconscionable advantage in trade and commerce.

"What then shall we say to these things? Shall we shrug our shoulders and acknowledge the bitter truth? Uncomfortably pass the buck to that remote impersonal scapegoat —Washington, D. C.?

"Shall we say this is all the result of some world-wide condition beyond our control or influence?

"Shall we come to meetings such as this and politely applaud the speaker when our emotions are stirred, and then settle back in comfortable lethargy, devoting our first allegiance and our best efforts to our own particular businesses or professions?

"Shall we loiter in the leisure of our five-day week and our ceramic conveniences and our comfortable procrastination?

"Shall we seek the popular compromise? Shall we speak softly in inoffensive generalities, afraid to voice our principles for fear of offending?

"Shall we all point in unison to the hillside where the pretty daffodils grow, for fear some faint-hearted might falter on the craggy slopes of reality?"

Goldwater in 1959 was not faint-hearted; and, where he
spoke, his sober indictment of the welfare state brought more
than applause. It produced action by citizens. Republicans
began to find new reasons for being Republican.

There is an old saying that men elected to high office
either grow or swell. Goldwater grew in understanding without suffering any loss of his warm personal involvement with
people.

From a campaign manager's standpoint, Goldwater is
almost the perfect candidate. He does his homework, is
never arbitrary or capricious, is not given to making last-
minute changes or altering pre-determined campaign
strategy. When he solicits an opinion, it is because he intends
to profit from that opinion, and he gives his advisors a full
hearing.

One Goldwater characteristic, however, can bring grey
hair to the head of the most experienced advance man.
After a speech or in a crowd, where individuals visit with
the Senator, schedules become meaningless. Barry is so
genuinely interested in what each person has to say he finds
it impossible to break away. This means that if the itinerary
calls for six meetings in one day, he is likely to be late for
every one except the first. At one point in the 1958 effort
this characteristic of Goldwater-the-campaigner almost produced a violent split between us.

We were in a northern Arizona town. The schedule had
called for a visit to an institution where the staff, represent-
ing about two hundred voters, were eager to see the Senator.
There had been no formal speech, but Barry's inability to
deny himself to anyone who wanted his ear made us thirty-
five minutes late when we finally broke away. The delay was
particularly aggravating, because more than one hundred

of the community's most influential citizens were gathered in a downtown hall in anticipation of the Senator's principal speech of the day.

Two-thirds of the way into town Barry, who was driving, suddenly turned off on a side street and parked in front of a very modest bungalow. He recognized the disapproval on my face and tried to counter it: "I know we're late, but they will wait a few minutes longer. This will take only a minute. Come on in." He bounded up the steps, knocked on the door, pushed it open, entered and began addressing the unseen occupant in warm and friendly terms.

A voice responded from the rear of the house. In a few minutes a pale, slender, middle-aged woman in a dressing-gown appeared in the hallway.

Barry embraced her. He sat down in the living room with the detached deliberation of a man who had nothing else on the schedule for that day. Barry commenced with inquiries about the woman's health, her children, their activity and their whereabouts. Together they recalled a hundred memories of childhood. They relived exploration of Indian ruins and student dances. When we finally left at the end of more than thirty minutes, my temper was at the breaking point. For this we had kept a hundred people waiting; for this we had risked alienating a solid segment of support we desperately needed.

There was a boulevard stop a quarter of a block away, and when we reached it and the car was halted, Barry turned to me and said, "I know we're late, Steve, but I had to do this. She is dying of cancer, and I could not be in this town without stopping, without letting her know that I hadn't forgotten. There aren't many left who care what happens to her, and I want her to know I care."

What can you say to a man whose concern for a friend of his youth outweighs the benefits he might receive from the waiting crowd?

The impact of Goldwater on the Republican Party in 1959 cannot be measured accurately. The year started with his election to the post of Chairman of the Senatorial Campaign Committee for the second time; a position he had held from 1954 to 1956.

When Congress reconvened in June 1959, Barry was aware that his fellow Republican Senators might again ask him to head this phase of Congressional campaign activity.

"They want me because I can raise money," he said, "and I'm not at all sure I want to take it. It's a heavy job, and I would like to coast and get caught up with my other duties."

When Jack Javits objected to Goldwater's becoming Chairman of the Campaign Committee on the ground that it would alienate liberals, Barry was infuriated.

The Republican Party, in Goldwater's opinion, was guilty of aping certain aspects of the New Deal. It was unrealistic to believe the bosses of union labor, who were very influential in the Democratic Party, would ever be anything less than resolute in their opposition to a Republican candidate. His election campaigns in Arizona and the Taft campaign in Ohio in 1950 had demonstrated that Republicans could win regardless of union boss opposition if they were boldly conservative.

A majority of the Senators who would be up for re-election in 1960 were conservative in their personal, political outlook. In addition to Case of New Jersey, they included Styles Bridges of New Hampshire, Leverett Saltonstall of Massachusetts, Karl Mundt of South Dakota, Andrew

Schoeppel of Kansas, Henry Dworshak of Idaho, Gordon Allott of Colorado, Carl Curtis of Nebraska, John Sherman Cooper of Kentucky, and Margaret Chase Smith of Maine.

Barry regarded the opposition of Javits as one more manifestation of liberal hostility toward a conservative cause. He had been lukewarm about the Chairmanship—now he determined to make a fight for it. Not much of a fight was required. After his smashing victory in Arizona, most of the Republican incumbents were eager for his advice and leadership.

Barry was invited to speak to one section of the Western Republican Conference convening at the Biltmore Hotel in Los Angeles, November 13, 1959. On the day before his scheduled appearance he had commitments in Arizona. We left Phoenix in the twin Bonanza at eleven o'clock for Prescott, a distance of about eighty-five miles by air, where Barry was to speak before a service club at noon. At two o'clock we left Prescott to fly to Safford, a farming community in the Gila Valley near the New Mexico border. Investigators from the Department of Interior were considering Safford as a possible location for an experimental saline-water conversion plant. State officials and representatives of the University of Arizona were scheduled to appear before the group that afternoon.

Shortly after five o'clock we departed from Safford for Los Angeles, a normal three-hour flight.

Weather broadcasts received en route indicated the Los Angeles airport was open, but when we reached a point fifty miles east of the great California metropolitan area, we encountered smog and poor visibility. West of the San Gorgonio Pass it was extremely difficult to see the ground. By this time it was dark, and Barry began to consider the advisability of making an instrument approach to Burbank, our destination.

We searched the Jepson * manual to find the instrument approach plate and discovered it was missing. Radio cleared us in VFR *; and, by dodging the patches of smog and relying on the dual omnis * in the aircraft for frequent position checks, we were finally able to enter the pattern * and land without incident.

We ordered a cab, gave instructions to service the airplane and began to think about dinner. It was well past eight o'clock, and Nelson Rockefeller was scheduled to make his major address before the Conference that evening.

When the cab arrived, we told the driver to take us to the Biltmore. He moved away from the ramp, stopped his cab, turned on the light, swung around on the front seat to face us. "Have either of you gentlemen ever been to the Biltmore before?" he asked. For a moment we were nonplussed. Had the Biltmore suddenly acquired some outrageous reputation? Had there been a fire or a catastrophe? In unison we both said, "Yes." The cabbie sighed with relief. "That's good, because this is my first day on the job, and I don't know how to find it." We told him if he could take us to downtown Los Angeles, we could take him to the Biltmore.

As we approached the Hill Street entrance, Barry suddenly turned to me and said, "Have you got any money?" One of Barry's delightful idiosyncracies is the fact that he habitually

---

* Jepson—publishers of rules for instrument approach, compass headings, altitudes, etc.

    VFR—visual flight rules

    Omnis—radio navigational aids

    Pattern—downwind, base, final headings and altitude required of aircraft landing.

forgets to take any cash with him. His friends laugh about it, and in Arizona he literally never needs any cash.

I produced a five dollar bill and said I'd pay the cabbie. When we entered the hotel, Barry, who had made the reservation, offered to register for both of us. He said it would save time.

There was no line at the desk, but with that infuriating deliberation which must be a studied talent of experienced hotel clerks the man at the desk managed somehow to take about fifteen minutes to assign our rooms. A bellboy took our two small bags, and we started upstairs, when Barry suddenly paused at the cashier's desk. "I'd better get some money," he offered by way of explanation.

I told him I had plenty. His reply was, "The night's young, and you might not have enough." While I waited with the bellboy, Barry wrote a check, offered it to the cashier, and then produced his billfold and began to display identification. Each time he offered a card the cashier solemnly shook her head. The hour was late, we were tired; it had been a long and somewhat difficult flight, and I could see the hackles begin to rise on the back of Barry's neck.

When I approached the window, I heard the hotel employee repeat what she must have been saying in each instance, "I'm sorry, don't you have a Biltmore Hotel credit card?"

The amount on the check was twenty-five dollars. Barry didn't have a Biltmore Hotel credit card, but he had dozens of other imposing identifications. The cashier refused them all.

"You'll have to see the manager," she said. Goldwater picked up the check, his billfold, his credit cards and stalked through the lobby to the manager's office. Five minutes later he returned with the assistant manager to a second cashier, who reluctantly gave him twenty-four dollars and eighty-five cents for his check. There was a fifteen-cent service charge.

On the way up in the elevator I told him he had forfeited some of my confidence. If a United States Senator can't cash a twenty-five dollar check, perhaps I should be more suspicious.

We freshened up and finally, after some indecision, agreed to go to the Biltmore Bowl, where Nelson Rockefeller was making his speech.

An earnest young man at the steps halted us. "We may not want to stay," Barry said, "but we'll just look in for a minute."

"I'm sorry, sir, but there's no more space. You can't go in."

"This is Senator Goldwater," I said.

"I'm sorry sir," the young man repeated. "There's no more space. You can't go in."

Barry turned his back on the doorman. "I think we'll get some dinner," he said. "This is not my night. We almost couldn't land at Burbank; the cab driver didn't know where the Biltmore Hotel was; it took twenty minutes to register in a twenty-five dollar a day room, and then I couldn't get a twenty-five dollar check cashed; now I can't get into my own meeting."

A Republican Party official, who had recognized Barry, came over and urged us not to be upset. "They're waiting for you, Senator. They have a chair on the platform for you," he said.

Rockefeller was in the middle of his speech. Barry was ushered down the side corridor to a room backstage, where he waited for almost twenty minutes while the New York Governor concluded his prepared remarks.

Earl Mazo, Nixon's biographer, who was covering Rockefeller's western tour for the New York *Herald Tribune,* appeared immensely pleased when the audience applauded at the conclusion of the Governor's speech.

This was followed by some organ music, one or two announcements by the chairman of the meeting, then Goldwater appeared from backstage and was introduced.

The crowd roared its approval with a demonstration of enthusiasm that dwarfed the Rockefeller applause. Barry's appearance broke up the meeting. Earl Mazo's face recorded his astonishment. He couldn't believe what he was seeing and hearing.

On the eastern seaboard skeptics argue that Goldwater has no popular appeal. This experienced newspaperman displayed a bewildered incredulity as he witnessed the crowd's reaction to Goldwater.

Governor Nelson Rockefeller had delivered an excellent speech. Half a dozen girls in scanty costumes were in the audience to give out Rockefeller buttons and Rockefeller literature; and the crowd had given him an appreciative handclap. They roared their approval of Barry.

CHAPTER XVIII

# NEW RESPONSIBILITY

LONG BEFORE the twenty-seventh National Convention
of the Republican Party was scheduled to open in Chicago in
1960, there were whispers of discontent in the party's secret
lodge-rooms. Nixon, the heir apparent, had the public support of most party leaders. In some states, early spring primaries made this official; in others, delegates had received
the word from their state chairmen and national committee
members.

The President's three serious illnesses created a situation
which made it almost impossible for competition to develop.
State chairmen and national committeemen, visiting the Capitol on official business, found the door to the Vice President's
office open. As one of them put it: "When we talked to
Nixon, we were all aware that he might be the President in
the next twenty-four hours."

Meade Alcorn had retired as chairman of the national committee, and been succeeded by the likeable, energetic Junior Senator from Kentucky, Thruston Morton. At committee headquarters on Eye Street in Washington, there was great activity but little progress. Ike's unwillingness to be a partisan President, combined with Sherman Adams' contempt of party regulars, had inflicted a near-fatal injury on what should have been a potent political organization.

National political parties live on patronage—not the kind of ward-heeling, bread-and-butter job distribution so necessary to city, county and state organizations—but the prestige appointments which are normally bestowed on big-time fund raisers and accomplished behind-the-scene vote getters. Men of importance, whose personal success in business or profession makes it impossible for the party to reward their loyalty in any other fashion, respond enthusiastically when they are consulted about the appointment of a federal judge or a customs collector or a member for one of the multitudinous federal commissions.

In other years, and under most administrations, such appointments were, without exception, cleared through the national committees of the party in power. Sherman Adams changed this. He ignored the national committee; he also ignored Republican senators and congressmen. He may have been an efficient administrator, ruling the White House staff with an iron hand, but as Goldwater expressed it, "He was a poor politician."

The undercurrent of dissatisfaction with some of the policy decisions of the Eisenhower Administration was not of sufficient proportion to be regarded as dangerous by party leaders. But in a number of states, there was a growing determination to get the party out of the middle of the road, and offer voters a meaningful choice between progressive Republican conservatism and the socialist state advocated by many Democrats.

Without seeking the position, Goldwater emerged as the leader of the conservative wing of the Republican Party. Demands for his book, *The Conscience of a Conservative*, exceeded all expectations. The popularity of his three-times-a-week column of political comment in *The Los Angeles Times* inspired many other papers to request it as well, and by June of 1960 the column, *How Do You Stand, Sir?*, was appearing in more than fifty newspapers across the land.

On the 17th of March, 1960, Barry went to the state convention of the Republican Party in South Carolina to serve as keynote speaker. His enthusiastic audience made him its unanimous choice for the 1960 Republican nomination and pledged him thirteen votes.

Greg Shorey, State Chairman of South Carolina, is a realistic politician. The handwriting on the wall was plain to him. Dick Nixon was going to be nominated. But he believed it would strengthen the party's chances in November if Nixon could be made aware of the determined sentiment of conservative Republicans. Barry agreed.

Goldwater intended to go to Chicago with a prepared statement withdrawing his name from consideration. But there was bargaining strength to be gained during those spring months by keeping his plans secret.

Barry wanted a conservative platform; he anticipated a determined effort on the part of eastern-seaboard, modern Republicans to cut the cloth of Republican promises after the pattern of the New Deal.

Dick Kleindienst, Arizona State Republican Chairman, and Congressman John Rhodes had committed the state's delegates to Nixon. Barry, who strongly preferred Nixon to

Rockefeller, had assured the Vice President of his personal support. But, if the plan to impress the convention with the numerical strength of the conservative segment of the party was to succeed, it was necessary to have Arizona's delegation pledged to Barry.

"I'd be like a scarecrow, left in the field after the corn was plowed under, if Arizona permitted South Carolina to carry the ball," Goldwater said.

To understand why the leaders of the Republican Party in Arizona weren't wildly enthusiastic about Goldwater as a native son candidate opposing the almost certain nomination of Nixon, it is necessary to recall the attitude of Sherman Adams after the Eisenhower election. Party officials going to the White House found an unsmiling Adams, who asked in icy tones, "Where were you before Chicago?"

Nixon understood what Barry was going to do and why he was doing it. He could afford to be generous, he had the nomination in his pocket. Nixon has never exhibited any petty vindictiveness and the cordial relations between Barry and the Vice President had not been affected by the action of the South Carolina Convention.

Arizona State Chairman Kleindienst, National Committeeman Colonel James C. Wood, and National Committeewoman Mrs. Emery C. Johnson were quick to recognize that the situation now required naming Barry as Arizona's favorite son. This was done at the State Convention on April 23, and Goldwater had twenty-seven official, pledged delegates, adding the fourteen of his home state to the thirteen from South Carolina.

Numerous enthusiastic, but unofficial, Goldwater-for-President Committees were formed. Aubrey Barker, Chairman

of the Yuma County Arizona Republican Central Committee,
a union member and an employee of the telephone company,
left his job to head one of these valiant efforts. Barker, a political idealist, was never quite able to understand the difference between gaining popular support of Republicans
throughout the country and having official support of convention delegates.

In New Orleans the publishers of the *Independent American*, Kent Courtney and his wife Phoebe, jumped on the band
wagon and began to support the Goldwater candidacy. Extremists of all descriptions seized upon the situation to foster
their own ideas and objectives. The Goldwater image was
twisted and distorted. Barry was pictured as being violently
anti-Nixon, isolationist and an advocate of preventive war, a
man who wanted to turn back the calendar at least to 1929,
a stubborn, violent, defender of the *status quo,* and a tool of
big business intent on destroying unionism in the United
States.

During this period, Barry's patience was stretched to the
breaking point. The very people who claimed they wanted to
help were inflicting great injury on the sober, reasonable,
forward-looking kind of conservatism Goldwater actually expresses. It was during this period that he said frequently, "I
can deal with my enemies, but the Lord will have to protect
me from my friends."

Not all of his friends travelled under the publicity banners
of the extremists. Dedicated Republicans throughout the nation wrote thousands of letters of encouragement. Respected
members of the Bob Taft wing of the party advised caution.
They had learned from experience that a politician never
gains strength from taking a licking. At least nine hundred

votes were pledged to Nixon; any serious Goldwater contention for the nomination might be disastrous.

As Chairman of the Senatorial Campaign Committee, responsible for the election of ten incumbent Republican
senators, Barry quite naturally assumed that those in charge
of the convention would place some emphasis on the strategy
for Senate seats. Either the convention's arrangers felt otherwise or the Nixon staff was afraid to allow Goldwater any
position of prominence.

On Tuesday, July 19th, Barry moved into two rooms at the
Blackstone, installed Edna Coerver at an improvised desk,
and prepared to wait out the writing of the platform before
making his official withdrawal announcement.

Barry was scheduled to appear before the platform committee on Wednesday afternoon.

Goldwater's statement (see appendix) to the platform
committee called for a declaration of principles—solid, conservative principles.

In Arizona in 1958, the Republican Party had broken prec-
edent, thrown aside the hackneyed collection of promises,
and boldly offered a simple statement of political philosophy. The Democrats, caught off guard, tried to counter by
making a futile charge that a platform was not a platform
unless it contained specific legislation and administrative suggestions. They pretended shock at inadequacies in the Republican statement. Election results indicate the voters
understood.

John Haugh, a member of the Arizona delegation from
Tucson and an experienced state legislator, and Arlene Pate,
a brilliant and attractive woman from Winslow, were the two
Arizona representatives on the platform committee. They

were being pressured by the Nixon-Rockefeller forces to approve federal-aid to-education and to promise general expansion of federal benefits.*

Charles Percy ** of Chicago, an experienced presiding officer with great charm and tact, was chairman of the platform committee. Percy had every right to expect prompt committee approval of the suggestions which had been unofficially advanced by the Nixon group. But the delegates had other ideas. The rest of the convention may have been a cut-and-dried affair, but the framing of the platform was a determined contest of wills between the conservatives and the liberals.

Time for writing the platform had to be extended. On one occasion deliberations were adjourned until the Chairman could bring in direct word from the Vice President. The upsetting news of Saturday, July 23, came within a hair of turning the platform committee deliberations into a full scale test of strength between conservative and liberal Republicans.

Barry had just been introduced to speak to the National Finance Committee, gathered in a second floor ballroom of the Hilton, when an urgent message from Len Hall interrupted.

The bomb which burst on Republican Chicago was the

---

* Dr. Ernest L. Wilkinson, President of Brigham Young University in Utah, took a poll of the delegates following the convention. Results were published in February and March of 1961 by the BYU Press. 1331 ballots were sent out to delegates. On school construction, 149 in favor, 698 against; on teachers salaries, 23 favored, 827 against.

** Charles Percy, President of the Bell and Howell Company, served in 1959 and 1960 as Chairman of the Republican Committee on Program and Progress. The committee was created by President Eisenhower and commissioned to establish Republican goals. The writer of this biography was also a member of that committee named by the Republican incumbent President.

first wire service story reporting Nixon's unscheduled visit to Rockefeller in New York. Many delegates, who until that moment had displayed some semblance of enthusiasm, exploded in anger. The undercover contest between the social welfare proposals of Nelson Rockefeller and basic Republican conservatism was exposed. The corpse everyone had pretended was buried came to life.

Len Hall, who was, nominally at least, Nixon's campaign manager, had received no advance information on the meeting between the Governor and the Vice President.

If Rockefeller had gone to Washington, the visit would have attracted little attention. The fact that Nixon had gone to New York was interpreted as a gesture of appeasement, if not capitulation.

Barry, who had tentatively scheduled a news conference for ten o'clock that day to read his prepared announcement withdrawing his name from consideration, stuffed the statement into his pocket and, in an off-the-cuff interview, described the Nixon-Rockefeller meeting as an "American Munich."

Even the most sober, objective Goldwater backers began to urge Barry to make a serious contest for the nomination. Whatever Nixon had hoped to accomplish by the midnight visit appears in retrospect to have actually planted the seeds for his ultimate defeat.

When details of the agreement between Rockefeller and Nixon reached Chicago, it became possible to identify the extent of the Nixon concessions. They amounted not so much to a shift in position as to a shift in emphasis. But the Midwesterners and the Pacific Coasters and the delegations from the South read in that agreement an end to their hopes for a strongly worded conservative platform.

The Texas delegation, which had come to Chicago pledged to Nixon, started to re-examine the extent of that commitment. State Chairman Thad Hutcheson and National Committeeman Albert B. Fay asked Goldwater to appear before the delegation.

The Arizona group began to take its favorite son candidate seriously. In dozens of state headquarters angry delegates demanded to be released from their earlier commitments. Telephone lines to Barry's Blackstone Hotel headquarters were jammed. The current issue of *Newsweek* on the stands contained Barry's advice to the party on how Republicans could win in 1960. (See appendix.) Students-for-Goldwater organized a parade; and the convention, which promised to be a "no contest" affair at dawn on Saturday, was suddenly infected with bitter controversy.

Goldwater, the principal character in all this drama, managed to maintain a detached attitude. The convention was still committed to Nixon beyond any possibility of an upset; but if three hundred Goldwater votes could be found, if three hundred delegates would stand by their guns and voice their protest, it would make a difference.

On Friday afternoon Goldwater had been casually informed by the committee-on-arrangements that he was expected to make a speech and introduce the Senatorial candidates on Monday night. Goldwater's private response to the invitation was, "Nice of them to tell me so far in advance."

Sunday was spent on the speech. Regardless of what else happened, Goldwater was determined to exploit every possible opportunity to enlist support for his incumbent Senators.

"Nothing is more deadly," he said, "than having a group of candidates on a platform, each eager to be seen by the camera and to hold the microphone as long as possible. Let's do it differently. Let's have the candidates in their own delegations, surrounded by their own enthusiastic supporters. Let's give the people of the nation, who watch this show on television, an exciting picture."

It was a good idea. At first the arrangements committee said it was impossible, but when the television networks were contacted directly, they agreed with enthusiasm.

Let someone else hunt for delegates and worry about the presidential nomination. Barry determined to use his time on this opening convention night to raise again the banner of a conservative Republican philosophy, to challenge the faint-hearted, to confront the "me-too-ers." Television cameras were cued in to pick up the candidates on the floor in their own state delegations.

At 7:18 that Monday night, Chairman Morton gavelled the convention to order. When the preliminaries were over, that doughty, courageous Republican, former-President Herbert Hoover, made a ringing and conservative address. The crowd arose and applauded; but when the chairman announced the introduction of Senator Goldwater, the delegates seized their banners and paraded the aisles in a demonstration of enthusiasm which would not be put down, despite the pleas of the chairman and the speaker. After a full eight minutes of this testimony to his popularity, Goldwater began:

"Mr. Chairman, my fellow Americans: you and I, as members of the Republican Party and delegates to this 1960 Republican Convention, are participating in decisions of great importance.

"Let us then, as Republicans, apply the test of conscience to our every act.

"Let us bring to this task the dedication and devotion of those who lived and died that we might be free.

"I want to talk to you tonight about the heart and soul of our historic party.

"I want to talk to you about the local and state candidates, who will go back to their homes after this convention and once again take up, with self-sacrifice and devotion, their great task which gives this party of ours its substance and vigor.

"Now, after the fanfare is over, these men and women, who share our beliefs in the divine nature of man and his great destiny, will carry the Republican message to every corner of this nation.

"The true Republican philosophy is a dynamic, compelling doctrine dealing with the full nature of man and not with his material needs alone. It is the living unquenchable spirit of the American Revolution. The touchstone is freedom, the goals the improvement of both man and his society, the nurturing of intellectual and spiritual capacity, the expansion of creative opportunity, and the perpetuation of that concept of limited government which provides a climate for maximum social and individual progress.

"Never before in the history of this Republic has the wisdom of the founding fathers of this nation been more apparent. They speak directly to the problem before us. Let us give heed to their counsel. We must not be lured by a lust for novelty.

"We dare not let ourselves become so fascinated by so-called bold programs that we forget soundness is more important than a superficial thing they call boldness.

"The New Deal has now become the New Frontier. A new slogan to dress up a shopworn, outmoded, outworn idea.

"In establishing the division of powers of the federal government, in providing for the delegation of authority implicit in the establishment of an executive, legislative, and judicial branch, the founders of this nation gave to us a system magnificently calculated to best serve the governmental needs of free men.

"This is no time for small disputes. Well-intentioned men of good motive are engaged in serious debate.

"Are men as responsible individuals to be free to fashion their own destiny?

"Shall mankind be condemned to exist as dependent servants of an all-powerful central government?

"In the halls of Congress, America must face and overcome these forces and these destructive ideas, which threaten to make men the slaves of concepts and doctrines which deny freedom and refute the dignity of the individual.

"We must keep alive—we must support—the one system of government which in our world today holds man's best hope for enduring peace and continuing progress.

"In our pre-convention deliberations we have discovered some honest and sincere differences of opinion. Republican voices have been raised in question against the adoption of words and phrases which in their opinion fail to give room for an expression of important viewpoints within our party.

"Now, what has gone on here in Chicago has been a demonstration of our serious intent to present to this nation a Republican Party capable of uniting divergent viewpoints and presenting to the nation a true Republican philosophy, dedicated to the preservation of the eternal values of our society.

"The Republican members of Congress are the articulate instruments of this philosophy. It is through their actions and their votes on legislative matters that we, the Republican Party, will express our philosophy that man has a soul as well as a stomach.

"The prophets of the Radical Liberal Left continue to offer only one solution to the problems which confront us. They tell us again and again and again we should spend our way out of trouble and spend our way into a better tomorrow.

"Now we need Republicans in the Congress to protect this nation against the reckless spenders.

"And what of the clear and unmistakable intention of Russia to conquer the free world?

"When the apostles of appeasement attempt to persuade us to accept piece-meal surrender in a timid refusal to face reality, we need Republicans in the Congress to protect this nation.

"When the apostles of appeasement continue their attempts to limit the development of new and better nuclear weapons systems, we need Republicans in the Congress to protect this nation.

"And when those who would persuade us to plunge into disarmament without adequate inspection pursue their reckless course, we need Republicans in the Congress whose goal is victory, not a stalemate.

"I might say, in a National Convention such as this, the spotlight is focused almost entirely upon the party's nominee for President and Vice President. This is important, but if we allow our attentions to be concentrated entirely upon these two candidates, we are forgetting that the President and Vice President can not do their jobs without the loyal support of loyal Republican members of Congress.

"As an American who loves this Republic and as a member of the Senate, I am committed to the Republican philosophy and to the Republican candidates.

"It is my belief the people of this land will return a Republican administration to office in 1960, and I shall work to that end, but I might suggest in all seriousness that you and I will not have discharged our full responsibility unless we also return an effective Republican Congress.

"I would not imply that our party is the repository of all virtue, that only Republicans can see the truth, that only Republicans serve noble motives, but I must insist that those in control of the Democratic Party through their platform have announced their total commitment to what I regard as a lopsided concept of man which puts Americans in a shameful position of everlasting dependence upon the state.

"I have visited the people in the cities and the towns and states of our nation, and I can tell you the men and women of America face the future with courage. They are eager to accept their responsibilities; they are determined to work and sacrifice to defend our freedom.

"It is our task as delegates to this 1960 Republican Convention to make certain the American voter is provided with an opportunity to make a meaningful choice between the two philosophies competing today for acceptance in our world, the philosophy of the *stomach* or the philosophy of the *whole man*.

"These men and women—these Republican candidates for the Senate—are your front line troops to represent your ideas, your principles. Their victories in November will be your victory. Through them you will shape destiny for your children."

As cameras darted around the room to settle on each candidate in turn, the delegates voiced their unlimited endorsement of that concept of government outlined in such magnificent, sharp relief by the Senator from Arizona.

CHAPTER **XIX**

# THE 1960 REPUBLICAN CONVENTION

T HE enthusiastic response by the delegates to Barry's brief statement of Monday night inspired his followers to double their efforts. There was no formal organization, no Goldwater-for-President headquarters, no disciplined teams methodically wooing each delegate, but there was earnest hope in the hearts of conservative volunteers.

The Texas delegation wrestled with its conscience from midnight Monday to midnight Tuesday and found it impossible to stay committed formally to Richard Nixon. The delegates were released to vote their own decisions.

Privately, hundreds of Republican delegates, perhaps the majority of those in Chicago, expressed their preference for Barry. The plight of the Wisconsin group was typical. As a result of party rules and Wisconsin state law, they were committed to continue voting for Richard Nixon until the convention was over. Indiana and Ohio were likewise legally and morally bound. Some delegations would be free to switch on the second or third ballot; but there was not going to be a third ballot, or a second ballot.

By midnight Tuesday 278 delegates had promised their first ballot vote to Goldwater. Those who are versed in the habits of nominating conventions will recognize that for a man who had not campaigned, who did not consider himself a candidate and who had no headquarters, or formal organization, this was a tremendous display of strength.

Members of the Arizona delegation, from its Chairman, Governor Paul Fannin, down to the last alternate, urged Barry to remain in the contest, to let the votes be counted. State Chairman Greg Shorey of South Carolina, and numerous influential delegates from Texas, chimed in and supported the pleas of the delegates from Barry's native state. A group of Young Republicans-for-Goldwater, headed by Bob Croll, staged a rally in downtown Chicago and begged for the privilege of participating in a demonstration at Convention Hall.

Barry was caught up in a sea of emotion, supported by the strong convictions of his conservative admirers. No man can pretend indifference when a substantial number of his fellow citizens make him their choice for the office of President of the United States.

In the background, however, beyond the rosy clouds of enthusiasm, the cold reality of numbers demanded caution. Many of the delegates, who had promised first ballot support, were from states following New York in the alphabetical roll call. And either just before or just after New York cast its ninety-six votes for Nixon, the Vice President would become, in fact, the nominee of the Republican Convention. It would require a reckless kind of political courage to stand in that hall on Wednesday night and vote for Goldwater, an assured loser, against Nixon, already the winner.

On Wednesday morning in downtown Chicago all of the 278 Goldwater delegates were resolute in their determination to support this forthright conservative, who had captured the imagination of the convention. But on Wednesday night, in the spotlight of the arena, fully aware of the possibility of punishment at the hands of the victorious nominee, how could any man hold the delegates to their Wednesday morning promise?

In the southern states, where the party lives on national patronage and little else, it would be political suicide for party leaders to vote against the man who had already been nominated for President.

Barry went before the delegations formally pledged to him, outlined the practical probability, and asked that his name not be put before the convention. The delegates refused to be silenced. They had selected their champion, and they had earned the right to express their sentiment for Goldwater, formally and officially, before the other delegates, in front of the television cameras. Their resentment against the cut-and-dried aspects of the convention strengthened their resolve, and Goldwater found it impossible to turn the tide.

At noon Wednesday Greg Shorey of South Carolina and Paul Fannin of Arizona simultaneously announced to the reporters that Goldwater's name would be placed in nomination that evening, and faithful followers shouted their joy. A formal request was made to those in charge of the convention for permission to bring demonstrators on the floor from outside the arena. After some delay the Goldwater supporters were promised 3,000 tickets.

The Yuma (Arizona) Indian Band, which had been

brought to Chicago by one of the many Goldwater-for-President groups, was selected to add music and noise to what these earnest Republicans believed was their best opportunity to reveal to the national party the conservative sentiment from the grass roots across the nation.

Barry returned to his rooms in the Blackstone and began to prepare his speech, asking formally that his name be withdrawn. The nomination, which his friends insisted on making, the seconding speeches—and dozens of Republicans were clamoring for the privilege of seconding the nomination—the demonstration, all this could be done without inflicting any wounds, without presenting any distorted reflection of conservative strength. But the realities of practical politics were clear in Barry's mind. If he left his name before the convention, it would be a defeat for the cause he served, and he would be acquiescing to an action which would place his friends in jeopardy. There was no possibility of winning a substantial victory, and there was great probability of suffering a disastrous defeat. Under the assault of the well-organized Nixon steamroller, the final count might very well be flattened to the 27 delegates pledged to him before the convention opened.

Barry's resolve was strengthened when word came from the Young Republicans-for-Goldwater that 3,000 demonstration tickets had been received, but they were tickets for Thursday, not Wednesday. This could have been an honest error made in the confusion and great disorder which surrounded headquarters in the Hilton. It also could have been deliberate.

The tickets were returned and finally replaced with admission passes for Wednesday night. As things turned out, it would have made no difference, for the ushers at the arena refused to honor any of the tickets held by the Goldwater demonstrators.

It is extremely doubtful that Nixon in his downtown hotel had any knowledge of this attempt to suppress the zeal of the Goldwater supporters. Originally the National Committee had arranged for forty-five hours of television coverage; but the lack-luster and, at times, boring pictures released from the Democratic Convention in Los Angeles, had prompted the committee to reduce its television commitment to less than twenty hours. No time had been allotted for a Goldwater demonstration, and as one delegate expressed it— "the convention was run for the television coverage and the convenience of the television commentators." Every second was scheduled, and veteran Republican Convention producer George Murphy was responsible for the show.

Long after the convention closed, Gregory Shorey, Chairman of the South Carolina delegation expressed his opinion to me in these words: "The delegates might just as well have sent their votes to Chicago by carrier pigeon, for all the good it did us to be there. The nomination was greased, the acceptance of the platform was oiled, the delegates came—not to deliberate, but to acquiesce. We were there as window dressers. We were told when to stand up, when to sit down, when to applaud and when to keep still. The aisles were jammed with the staffs of the television networks, who rudely interrupted whenever it pleased them to do so. It was their show and they knew it. The stockyards was an appropriate setting—we were the prize cattle."

The Honorable Charles Halleck of Indiana, Permanent Chairman of the Convention, gavelled the delegates to order at 7:14 P.M. on the night of Wednesday, July 27th. The formal preliminaries consumed considerable time. Then

Charles Percy made his "visual aid" presentation of the Republican platform. This was followed by the introduction of Thomas Dewey and his speech applauding the Eisenhower Administration. The minutes dragged by until, finally, the chairman offered the delegates an opportunity to perform the task which had brought them to Chicago. Before the roll call of the states began, Chairman Halleck proposed and passed a rule limiting seconding speeches to four in number and five minutes in length.

Claude Vardaman of Alabama announced his state was yielding to Oregon, in order that Governor Hatfield might nominate Dick Nixon. Alaska passed and the State Chairman of Arizona announced that Governor Paul Fannin was on the platform for the purpose of making a nomination for the office of President.

Governor Hatfield's speech was short; it should have been. His job was merely to ink the rubber stamp which would be used to make formal a foregone conclusion. Kuchel of California, Del Sesto of Rhode Island, Mrs. Jewel Rogers of Illinois, and young Bob Taft, followed by John Roosevelt of New York, Mrs. Andrew Williams of Washington, Robert L. Gavin of North Carolina, and Jacob Javits of New York made their seconding speeches. There were eight in all. Either the chairman couldn't count or deliberately ignored the rule just proposed and passed, limiting seconding speeches to four. The rule did not apply in the case of Mr. Nixon.

Governor Paul Fannin, tall and determined, born in the mountains of Kentucky, reared from childhood in Arizona, approached the microphone. Fannin, who is respected for his administrative ability, had never appeared before so large an audience as on this Wednesday night, and he was magnificent.

"Mr. Chairman, fellow Republicans, my fellow Americans, the action I shall take here tonight is directly contrary to the wishes of a man who has been my friend since childhood. As all of you know, at ten o'clock this morning the man whom I shall place in nomination specifically recommended against such action. In any other situation I would feel compelled to accept his decision without question, but this is not an ordinary situation. The Arizona delegation, after careful deliberation, was unanimous in its insistence that I carry out this responsibility.

"Tens of thousands of telegrams have been received by delegates to this convention demanding that this action be taken.

"All across the broad face of America the people are pleading that their voices be raised in this convention to express their approval of and their gratitude to this man.

"By his articulate, honest devotion to this conservative philosophy of government he has been thrust into a position of unquestioned leadership, as the voice of conscience speaking for the conservatives of this nation.

"Consult your recent memories. The declarations before this convention—the speeches and the speakers—have been most vociferously applauded and approved when they have voiced their commitment to the conservative doctrines of a strong free nation, supported by responsible individual citizens moving forward together under the leadership of governmental theories calculated to satisfy the noble spiritual aspirations of man, as well as to meet his material requirements.

"His efforts and his energies have been devoted to strengthening the Republican Party, and Republicans in every state of our union can testify to the effectiveness of his efforts.

"He is dedicated to the preservation of our constitutional Republic.

"He has supported the leaders of our nation under our Party.

"He has helped to advance the programs of our Party.

"His name must be presented to this convention as a demonstration that we are assembled to serve the cause of freedom as responsible individual representatives of the Republican Party."

Then Fannin outlined Goldwater's successes as a campaigner in 1952 and again in 1958, describing him as the number one target of union bosses and the national Democratic Party.

"My friends, I am persuaded," Fannin said, "there is a destiny in the affairs of men and of nations. There are moments in history when power is given to a man to do what is right for his fellowmen, when Divine Providence intervenes, that God's plans for his creation may be carried out. Mr. Chairman, I place in nomination for the office of President of the United States a man with the courage of heroes, United States Senator Barry Goldwater of Arizona."

The applause was thunderous. All over the convention hall delegates raised their banners and broke into the aisles.

The Arizona delegation was seated on the left side of the hall directly in front of the podium; and the state's standard, in the hands of its chairman, Dick Kleindienst, moved into the aisle. The ushers led the demonstrators forward toward the front of the platform, and then turned the tide to the left. At the first side aisle a solid phalanx of ushers kept saying, "Hurry up, go this way, Barry wants you to go this way, go straight ahead." The indicated aisle led to the front of the hall beside the platform and to a door. When the door opened, the Arizona delegation found itself outside the arena, where still more ushers were giving directions: "Go outside to the back of the hall and come in the rear door."

The rear door was blocked by a solid mass of spectators and ushers; the ushers, with arms locked, refused to permit admission to the floor.

"No one goes in here," they said. "No one goes in here. You'll have to stay off the floor." I know what they said, for I was in that crowd. Big Bill Turner, a delegate from Arizona, was at my side and he knew the rules.

"You can't keep us off the floor, we're delegates," he said. And with a mighty shove, we broke through the resisting ushers.

Not all of the Arizona delegates were so fortunate, and not a single non-delegate, not one lone member of the 3,000 Goldwater supporters holding demonstration tickets, was permitted on the floor. The Indian Band from Yuma played outside to a crowd estimated at 5,000. The official band within the arena and the organ player were mute. There was no music to whip up enthusiasm.

On the platform George Murphy urged the permanent chairman to quiet the demonstrators; finally he appealed to Barry. "We're running overtime. This must be stopped."

Bruce Alger of Texas made the first seconding speech, followed by Greg Shorey of South Carolina, L. R. Houck of South Dakota, and Congressman John Rhodes of Arizona.

The chairman had rediscovered the rule. There were to be only four seconding speeches.

Senator Barry Goldwater, his head held high, his eyes on the future of the nation, came to the microphone.

"Thank you, Mr. Chairman, delegates to the Convention and fellow Republicans. I respectfully ask the chairman to withdraw my name from the nomination." There was an angry cry of "no, no."

Barry continued: "Please. I release my delegations from their pledge to me, and, while I am not a delegate, I would suggest they give these votes to Richard Nixon.

"Now, Mr. Chairman, with your kind permission and indulgence, as a conservative Republican I would like to make a few statements that will not take more than a few moments, and I think might help in this coming election.

"We are conservatives. This great Republican Party is our historic house. This is our home."

Then, with great conviction, Goldwater outlined the necessity for a Republican Party united in its opposition to the welfare state programs of the Democrats. He rebuked the conservatives who, in the past, had stayed home and refused their support to Republicans because of their dissatisfaction with a platform which must necessarily be a compromise of viewpoints. He underscored the demonstration of the conservative sentiments just concluded. And then he said:

"This country is too important for anyone's feelings. This country, and its majesty, is too great for any man, be he Conservative or Liberal, to stay home and not work just because he doesn't agree. Let's grow up, Conservatives. We want to take this party back, and I think some day we can. Let's get to work. I am a Conservative, and I am going to devote all my time from now until November to electing Republicans from the top of the ticket to the bottom of the ticket. I call upon my fellow Conservatives to do the same."

It was all over. Now the actors could return to their scripts and play the roles assigned to them. The roll call of the states began.

Peggy Goldwater and her daughter Peggy, Jr., in their box on the left side of the arena, wiped the tears from their eyes. Once more Barry "had paid the rent."

It is interesting to read the journal of the proceedings of that convention.* Following an account of the Hatfield speech nominating Dick Nixon, the official recorder notes: "there followed a great demonstration lasting seventeen minutes."

After the Fannin speech there is this sentence in brackets: "[At the conclusion of Governor Fannin's address there were cheers and applause, and a demonstration lasting approximately eleven minutes.]"

Thousands of outsiders came to the floor bearing their neat, printed placards of support for Dick Nixon. The official music in the arena screamed in high voice and no one on the platform attempted to halt the display.

The shouting and marching for Goldwater, despite the ushers who steered the demonstrators outside the hall, despite their refusal to honor convention demonstrator passes held by the Goldwater adherents who were not delegates, despite the lack of any music, could not be quelled before eleven minutes had passed.

On the clock the score was seventeen to eleven, but the clock, like the words in the journal, stands convicted of hypocrisy. Perhaps it was necessary, for had the ushers honored those passes, if they had failed in their efforts to get Goldwater delegates off the floor and outside the hall, the nation

---

* The Twenty-Seventh Republican National Convention, Chicago 1960, published by the Republican National Committee.

would have witnessed the ridiculous spectacle of a demonstration for a man who could not be nominated, lasting far longer than the planned demonstration for a candidate who had been selected long before the delegates assembled.

CHAPTER **XX**

## "YOU KNOW WHERE HE STANDS"

**G**OLDWATER meant what he said in Chicago. There was no sulking in the tent for this conservative. He made a hundred and twenty-six speeches in twenty-six states between July 28 and November 8, 1960; he travelled almost as far as, and a good deal faster than, the nominees; and he suffered without complaint the bitter criticism of the far, frantic right.

Kent Courtney and Dan Smoot sent out reports purporting to document a Goldwater sellout in Chicago. The liberal press treated him like a stingless hornet buzzing harmlessly around the heads of their heroes.

When it was all over, when the Senator from Massachusetts was elected by a majority of less than 113,000 votes, Barry returned briefly to his hilltop home to gather strength for a continuing struggle against those who would make the central state supreme.

Giveaways and handouts and unearned subsidies win the

cheers of the unthinking crowd. The noble phrases employed by the advocates of the welfare state have great appeal: human rights above property rights, adequate medical care for the valiant senior citizens. Deplorable public want is contrasted with selfish private opulence, college educations are proposed for all regardless of the economic position of parents. Help for the backward nations is Christian charity, that's all—Christian charity enforced by the iron hand of the federal tax collector.

The new President made a ringing speech in which he said: "Ask not what the government can do for you, ask what you can do for the government." And then, in rapid succession, his "voices" in Congress introduced legislation calling for fifteen or twenty billion dollars in additional federal handouts of one sort or another.

Goldwater issued what has been called a manifesto,* in which he asked his colleagues to consider the morality of legislation which takes by force from the producers of the United States and redistributes by bureaucratic decree.

The incumbent Republican Senators, who face election or defeat in 1962, unanimously requested Barry once more to head their Senatorial Campaign Committee. And all across the land men and women, who heretofore had been indifferent, unaware, too preoccupied with their own lives to take much interest in politics, solicited the advice of the young Senator from Arizona. His office was almost buried under a deluge of mail. Requests for personal appearances amounted to an average of more than one hundred each week.**

Because Barry accepted as many as possible, these oppor-

---

* A Statement of Proposed Republican Principles, Programs, and Objectives—Senate speech, Wednesday, January 11, 1961.

** See appendix for typical requests.

tunities to speak have been interpreted by liberal writers as an indication that Goldwater is campaigning for the Republican nomination in 1964. A sizable group of influential party leaders, state chairmen, national committeemen and committeewomen have written letters to the Senator, urging him to permit them to implement an active campaign for delegates to the 1964 convention.

At least once each week Barry is required, by questioners who demand an answer, to repeat his statement of position:

"I'm not seeking the nomination. I'm not seeking convention delegates. I'm not a candidate, and I do not regard myself as a potential candidate. All my efforts are dedicated to the election of Republicans to the Congress."

No political crystal ball can accurately predict the temper of this nation and its sovereign citizens three years in advance. Nor can any one of those individual citizens definitely describe what his own action might be when confronted with the realities of 1964.

In most states you will find Republicans and some Democrats who believe Barry will be elected President in 1964 if the Republicans nominate him. Experienced political observers in Arizona, who have followed Barry's two campaigns, concede Goldwater's ability to attract voter support; they doubt he will be nominated. Dick Herman of Omaha, Nebraska, who is close to Senator Carl Curtis and is regarded as a knowledgeable and powerful Republican politician, argues that advance organization, money and "deals" determine the party's nominee. As proof of this he offers the results of both the Democrat and Republican Party conventions since 1940.

Barry has no agents in the field seeking delegates. He has no nationwide organization; no campaign kitty. And when

friends urge him to take action now, he invariably changes
the subject.

In the great State of Texas the Goldwater conservatives
flexed their muscles, took their friends and neighbors to the
polls and elected a Republican, John Tower, to the Senate—
the first Republican to be so elected in Texas for over seventy
years.

"A political accident," say Goldwater critics.

"A result of local conditions," is the way Democrats in
Washington describe it.

"Meaningless and unreliable as a basis for predicting what
the people of the nation might do," say the supporters of
Nelson Rockefeller.

But consider the actual fact: a young college professor,
running as a Goldwater Republican, received the majority of
votes cast in the contest to decide the successor to Lyndon B.
Johnson.

The editors of *Fortune* * surveyed the scene from atop
their pillar of erudition and produced a profile on Goldwater.
"A nice, attractive, unusual fellow, but of course he can't
win." An interesting appraisal, particularly when reviewed
against the background of Barry's flat statement that he's not
seeking nomination.

*Time* put Barry on the cover,** and a number of other
publications *** did "thought pieces" to enable their readers
to evaluate the Arizona Senator, who had become such hot
news copy.

In the pages of *Coronet* magazine for July 1961, Mr. William Buckley, himself a stalwart conservative, offered a piece

---

* May, 1961.
** June 23, 1961.
*** *Newsweek,* August 1, 1961; *U.S. News and World Report,* August 7,
1961; *Progressive,* April, 1961, etc.

which faced the issue squarely: *What Kind of a President Would Goldwater Make?*

If people are in doubt as to what kind of a President Barry Goldwater would make, surely it is only because they have failed to follow his career, to read his public statements, and do not know of his Senate speeches.

Distortions, misquotes, single sentences out of context, all have been widely circulated and are eagerly seized upon by Barry's opponents: from liberal-minded college professors, who long to build heaven-on-earth for man, to tough-minded, power-seeking labor union bosses, who intend to lay out the streets and to control the traffic signals when heaven is established.*

Following the great clamor over the statement of principles issued by the city fathers of Newburgh, New York, Herblock in the Washington *Post* depicted Goldwater as a bestial giant condemning newborn babies.

In Texas, a vice chairman of the Democratic Party of Arizona, launched an assault on Goldwater condemning those who believed in God and patriotism.** And in a Phoenix newspaper, Billy Stephens, chairman of the Maricopa County Democratic Party, professed to read in Barry's op-

---

* Douglas J. Stewart, Department of Classics, Cornell University in a letter to the Wall Street Journal said: "Goldwater, a la Cicero, wants change —a shift into reverse." Sam B. Goddard, Jr., Chairman, Arizona State Committee, in the July, 1961 issue of *Arizona Democrats* said: "We have also seen that roving Junior Senator and jet pilot roar into the Valley and tell a military audience at Luke Air Force Base that 'education, Park Avenue and communism are synonymous.' It's amazing what that Presidential bug does to people." In Los Angeles, preceding a speech to some college students, Barry said he couldn't understand why so many Harvard students accepted the Keynesian philosophy. Later on he spoke about the value of fraternities. The *Baltimore Catholic Review* quoted him as saying: "Where fraternities are not allowed communism flourishes." The wire service which circulated the story explained the reporter had confused Keynesian with communism.

** *Fort Worth Star Telegram*, July 19, 1961, Associated Press.

position to the unlimited confiscatory power of the federal Income Tax a desire to place the total burden of government on the little man through the imposition of a sales tax.*

Al Capp, whose newspaper column appears in twenty-five or thirty papers throughout the country, followed a course of tortuous logic to condemn Barry when he praised an American Legion Post for its independent efforts in erecting a new building.**

During the Senate election in Arizona, in 1958, even Barry's active enemies grudgingly expressed their admiration for his honesty and his frankness.

"I don't agree with him," they said, "but, by gosh, you know where he stands."

Following most of his public appearances, Goldwater asks for questions from his audience. His answers are not always popular, but they are invariably recognized as direct. Where most politicians seek to hedge their bets, to leave the door ajar, Goldwater slams the escape route shut behind him.

"Communism is the evil which threatens the world today. The imperialistic, rocket-rattling policies of Khrushchev are costing the American people at least fifty billion dollars a year. America must thrust aside the wishful thinking that Communism can be contained, and settle on a course calculated to produce victory. We must win the cold war."

Does this statement indicate that Barry is advocating a military attack on Soviet Russia? Far from it. What he does say is this: we must use the peaceful weapons at our command strategically, and we must use our military strength to insure the success of our non-military thrusts.

---

* *The Arizona Republic,* August 27, 1961.
** Al Capp column for release Thursday, June 22, 1961. (This column was printed in a Chicago paper the fourth week in August, 1961.)

The Russians have broken all but two of some fifty-odd agreements negotiated between the Communist bloc and the free-world nations since the end of World War I.

"What is left to negotiate?" says Barry. "And if we reached a settlement, how permanent would that settlement be? The Russians are determined to conquer the world. If we believe in freedom, we must be equally determined to halt that conquest."

Long before Khrushchev resumed nuclear testing in September of 1961, Goldwater was arguing for a build up of American military strength. In his suggestions before the platform committee, July 19, 1960, in Chicago, he said: "To our undying national shame there are those among us who would prefer to crawl on their bellies to Moscow rather than face the possibility of an atomic war.

"Our enemies are capitalizing on our inability or unwillingness to recognize the true implications of the cold war. Russia is determined to destroy our ideals and our ideas, and the tragedy of freedom is that so far they have been frighteningly successful.

"I am suggesting the Republican Party must determinedly maintain the most powerful military power in the world, and that we must be willing to use this military power—and our economic power—to defend the rights of American citizens and to defend American property.

"I am suggesting the first responsibility of the federal government is to defend freedom with all the force and power and resources at our command. I am suggesting that Russia is determined to achieve victory—that we have not been equally determined—and if Russia's ambition for world conquest will not be satisfied short of an aggressive war, then no amount of appeasement, no action short of surrender will satisfy the Russian ambition.

"We must not agree to further bans on nuclear testing. Let us resume testing now. If our emissaries can arrive at an enforceable agreement with the Russians, then it will be time to stop, but not until then.

"Castro's Cuba does not represent the aspirations of a majority of peace-loving Cuban citizens. His dictatorship is a Communist cancer, ninety miles from the continental United States. The Monroe Doctrine should be invoked and economic sanctions imposed. The attempt to overthrow Cuba would have succeeded," Barry believes, "if the United States had not withdrawn its promised air and sea support.*

"Until the United States once again demonstrates that it is strong enough to defend itself and its citizens against any military attack or verbal onslaught, we cannot hope to enjoy the respect of the rest of the world.

"Prestige is a meaningless word. Respect is meaningful. It can't be bought with giveaways or with milk and honey speeches. It is out of character for America to appear before the world as a repentant sinner, just because American ingenuity and American opportunity have enabled our people to earn for themselves a higher standard of living than is enjoyed by the natives of Pago Pago. America is great and productive because Americans are free—free to succeed, free to fail—and have always been willing to defend their freedom with their blood and their treasure."

Goldwater believes that if the thinking of those who say it is better to be Red than dead ever becomes the national outlook, Khrushchev will be ready to celebrate his world

---

* *Fortune* magazine, September, 1961.

victory. "Unless man is prepared to die to defend those eternal values to which he gives his allegiance, life will soon become a frustrating, meaningless, imposed existence."

To support his contention that American foreign policy must be built upon the determination for victory, Goldwater points to those few instances where the free world has stood firm and the Russians have backed down.

"Communism is a phony success story," he says, "and most of the people living under Communism today know this to be true. This tyranny has been imposed upon people by force; it has never been accepted by a majority with the right to choose.

"The Russians have made some notable accomplishments in science," Goldwater concedes. But, in his opinion, the invidious comparisons used by the Democratic candidate for President in the 1960 campaign gave a totally false reflection of Russian progress.

"They started from nothing forty-three years ago. Of course their percentage improvement is high, but starvation still stalks the people under Communism. Their steel capacity doesn't begin to equal that of the United States, let alone that of the free world nations. In housing and health and universal education they are decades behind us. And each time Khrushchev speaks, he admits this, because each new five-year or ten-year plan has as its goal 'catching up' with the United States. If Communism is so superior, if this is truly the historic wave of the future, why haven't they caught up now?"

The basis for Goldwater's conservative philosophy on domestic matters is his belief that liberty is indivisible. A man cannot be politically free and economically a slave. Private property is unimportant, in and of itself, but the right to possess private property is essential to individual freedom. To be worthy of freedom a man must be responsible, and when the centralized state attempts to relieve the individual of certain unpleasant responsibilities, it destroys human integrity. Man, as a child of God, must be permitted freedom of choice even to behave improvidently, without interference.

The critics of Goldwater, who maintain that Barry would do away with the federal income tax, abolish Social Security and unemployment insurance, and prune away the branches of federal government until nothing but a skeleton tree survive, simply have not been listening to him.

The present Social Security law holds forth a false promise to millions of unsuspecting citizens, and thus prepares the way for ultimate tragedy. It is not insurance. Continued payments cannot be made unless a constantly increasing force of youngsters continue their contributions and increase the present level of contributions. Goldwater is opposed to compulsory social security and opposed to maintaining the fiction that present benefits will permit a retired individual to live in dignity. He suggests that those presently under the program be allowed voluntarily to increase their contributions, in order to build up an ultimate benefit of perhaps $250 or $300 a month (about twice the present maximum). He also believes that benefits should, to some degree, reflect amounts contributed.

The present law provides that an individual, who has earned $4,800 in each year since 1959, is entitled to receive exactly the same amount as another individual who has made contributions for twenty-five years or longer. The inequity here is so obvious it requires no documentation.

Goldwater is far too wise to believe that present, or greatly curtailed, budgets could be supported if the federal income tax were abolished. He is strongly opposed to withholding tax provisions, which deprive an individual of the responsibility of paying his own tax, and which have resulted in a general state of ignorance about the amount of tax collected.

Barry says most people under questioning can name the exact amount of their take-home pay; very few can name the total amount of their salary. He believes the withholding tax is the anesthetic which has made it possible for the federal government to extract larger and larger tribute from the uninformed wage earners.

A graduated federal income tax was strongly advocated by Karl Marx as a weapon for destroying the free enterprise societies of the world.* It is praised by the uninformed as the most equitable means of financing government expenditures, because it is "based on ability to pay," and platform demagogues beat their breasts in sympathy for the low-income wage earner while patting themselves on the back for assessing multi-millionaires up to ninety percent of their income.

The sad truth, which Goldwater stresses, is the fact that eighty-five percent of all monies collected by the federal government on individual incomes is derived from the wage earners who fall into the lowest tax brackets.** The wealthy avail themselves of high-priced tax counsel and translate their earnings into long-term capital gains, or spin off their fortunes into tax-free foundations. Very few suffer from an effective tax rate of more than fifty percent. But this is sufficient to kill initiative.

---

* Communist Manifesto by Karl Marx, Gateway Edition, page 55—first rule advocated by Marx, abolition of private property.
** United States Treasury report on sources of income.

"The producers, the men with vision capable of forming new businesses and creating new jobs, weigh the risk against the gain. If they are successful, if they win, Uncle Sam will step in and claim fifty percent or more of their winnings. If they lose, the loss is theirs. What moral right does the federal government have to punish and penalize initiative and ability by confiscating so much more of the earnings of the man who is successful than they take from the man who lacks initiative or ability to demand a high income?" [*]

Goldwater believes there should be a gradual reduction in the present tax rates and an immediate increase in the allowance for exemptions. He knows this would bring a loud scream from the treasury officials, who, he says, invariably behave as though it were their money the people are spending. An increase in exemptions to one thousand dollars would still not compensate for the present inflated cost of living, but it would lessen the burden on thousands of American citizens and eliminate several million from the tax rolls. This, in turn, would permit the Internal Revenue Bureau to operate with fewer employees.

The proposals of federal aid-to-education are another dividing line which separates conservatives from welfare state socialists. Because he has opposed federal control and financing of public education, Barry has been described by his critics as opposed to adequate educational opportunities for American children. Goldwater fights increased federal financing for schools because he believes federal control must ultimately follow the federal purse, and that central control of education is inconsistent with the traditional American concept of freedom.

---

[*] Prescott, Arizona, June 1957.

Barry has said: "In modern times tyranny has commenced with regimentation in the classroom, with the removal of individual determination and with the substitution of mass or collective objectives."

To those who insist there is great need for additional funds with which to finance school construction, Goldwater has proposed legislation which would increase the availability of funds without involving federal aid.

"Taxpayers defeat school bond issues," Goldwater says, "because this is the only area where the individual citizen can still say 'no' to an increased tax grab, and overburdened taxpayers can be forgiven if they express their animosity for ever-increasing taxes in the only manner available to them."

The legislative proposal which Barry introduced [*] provides that any real property owner, who pays school taxes for construction, be permitted to deduct up to one hundred dollars as a direct tax credit against his federal income liability. Most school districts itemize charges, and the bond redemption interest portion of the school tax bill usually amounts to about twenty percent of the total school tax costs. By making this tax credit available, there would be an effective transfer of federal funds to local purposes, and the Washington middleman would be eliminated.

Patrons of the school districts would, Barry believes, still exercise prudent control over local school expenditures, but the tax credit would permit them to allocate this portion of their money to direct construction costs, without increasing their overall tax bill.

Lobbyists for federal aid-to-education, in Goldwater's opinion, confirmed his belief that what they desire is federal

---

[*] Educational Opportunities Act of 1961, introduced February 20, 1961.

control more than federal money, and they opposed this simple device, which would have provided all the money necessary, but would have eliminated federal authority and direct federal control.

Goldwater made his attitude toward state welfare crystal clear in the Newburgh dispute. Here the city fathers said: if you can't get a job and are on public relief, you may have the opportunity to earn the money you receive, by performing needed services for the municipality.

"It is horrible, un-American," cried the liberals.

"If you won't take a job when it is offered to you," said Newburgh officials "we won't ask your fellow citizens to continue to support you in idleness."

"Dreadful," said the liberals, but they reserved their greatest screams of protest for the simple Newburgh declaration in regard to unwed mothers: "Women, who have been receiving benefits because they are the mother of one or more illegitimate children, will not be given additional benefits if they have more illegitimate children."

"You are condemning the innocent babies," said the liberals, and Herblock drew his derogatory cartoon. The city fathers of Newburgh, who were supported in this attitude by Goldwater, did not say that public charity would not care for the child, and Barry has made this repeatedly clear.

"Of course the babies are not to be punished; but, for heaven's sake, let's stop rewarding loose and immoral women every time they give birth to an illegitimate child."

Barry Goldwater's fifty-two years of living testifies to his compassion for his fellow man. He is aware of the frailities of human nature; but he is opposed to a concept of government which encourages men to be weak, to be improvident, to be immoral.

"In fulfilling our Christian obligation to be charitable in all things, we must not eliminate those sanctions which have worked so well to support men in their quest for good. If government lets down the bars and gives its tacit approval to man's ignoble vices, society will soon follow suit, and our world will become a jungle of unrestrained selfishness."

Goldwater is opposed to the Christmas-basket type of foreign aid which characterized the foreign policy attitudes of both the Eisenhower and Truman administrations. Because he believes so strongly that man is meant to be free, the posture of the uncommitted nations who claim to be neutralist is unacceptable to him personally; and he cites the fact that Russian-designed Mig jet fighters, built in a lend-lease financed plant in Czechoslovakia, are now flying over Cuba, as proof of the folly of our hundred billion dollar fiasco.

"In one breath they tell us they are not trying to buy friends," Barry says. "In the next they tell us if we don't support every other nation on earth with our money, these emerging people will turn to Moscow. This is international bribery on a big scale; and people who can be bought don't stay bought. The superiority of freedom to slavery is apparent to everyone, and, in my judgement, the people of America have first call on the sympathies of the American government. If we had a nationwide referendum on the present foreign aid program, the international lobbyists who cram this down the throats of the American taxpayers would be snowed under by 'noes.'"

Goldwater believes the military assistance part of the foreign aid program should be continued. He also favors technical assistance and loans where there is assurance of repayment. Americans should be ready to help their neighbors who truly want to help themselves, but we have no moral right to contribute to the deterioration of our neighbors by continuing a systematic subsidy program which will be ultimately destructive.

If the purpose of foreign aid is to strengthen countries friendly to the United States—if the purpose of foreign aid is to defeat communism—then it is time to make this an effective instrument of American foreign policy rather than a grab bag of goodies opened to some of our enemies before we offer it to our friends.

Above and beyond everything else on this earth, Goldwater loves the land of his birth. His loyalty to the time-honored concepts of constitutional government has been demonstrated by his statements and actions on a thousand issues, both personal and public. He longs for a land where every child can enjoy the opportunities this new world gave to his peddler grandfather, and he is opposed to every restriction, every limitation, private or public, which infringes on the freedoms guaranteed by the U.S. Constitution.

The men of vision who have led the people on this earth toward freedom since man first emerged from the cave, have been sustained by their recognition of an almighty, supernatural, loving intelligence. Goldwater, who stands so tall before his fellow man, kneels before his God asking for the wisdom and the strength to serve in this painful pilgrimage to achieve God's intention for his creation:

"To do that which is right in Thy sight."

# APPENDIX

*Following is the text of Senator Goldwater's statement to the Republican Platform Committee, plus his suggested Declaration of Republican Principles, made in Chicago on July 19, 1960.*

*These expressions seem to give a clear-cut picture of the Senator's political philosophy.*

—THE EDITORS

In recent years, the platforms of political parties have become a catchall of ambiguous phrases, designed to please everyone and offend no one. They are loosely worded in order not to bind the party to any specific course of action.

Special interest pressure groups, combined with ambitious politicians eager to purchase votes, exert tremendous influence on platform committees—and the response is usually an attempt to placate all sides. The question is who will look to the best interest of the nation?

No successful political party, even when in possession of complete control of the House, the Senate and the Administration, has ever passed or attempted to pass all the legislation suggested by platform promises.

The American people have become cynically suspicious of political platforms, and I am suggesting that the Republican Party, in this year of national peril, would do well to discard discredited patterns of the past and offer to the people a declaration of principle.

If you will tell me what a man believes, if you will tell me those principles to which a man swears allegiance, I can predict, with reasonable accuracy, how this man will respond to any given situation. And I suggest the American people will be far more eager to place their destiny in the hands of a man who announces his beliefs and his principles than in the hands of a man who promises and promises and promises, knowing he cannot keep his promises.

I am suggesting the issue which we must decide is one of freedom or slavery. The world stands divided on this issue today.

Unfortunately, the challenge is not presented in such clearly defined and recognizable terms.

There are those among us in this nation who cherish the false notion that by accommodating the totalitarian doctrine of Communism we can continue to maintain the uneasy peace we have enjoyed since the end of World War II. There are also those among us who, when confronted with the ultimate choice, appear to prefer appeasement and piecemeal surrender of the rights and freedoms of man.

To our undying national shame, there are those among us who would prefer to crawl on their bellies to Moscow rather than to face the possibility of an atomic war.

Our enemies are capitalizing on our inability or unwillingness to recognize the true implications of the cold war. Russia is determined to destroy our ideals and our ideas. And the tragedy of freedom is that so far they have been frighteningly successful.

We must not agree to further bans on nuclear testing. Let us resume testing now. If our emissaries can arrive at an enforceable agreement with the Russians, then it will be time to stop, but not until then.

We must not agree to disarmament, as proposed by our enemies, with the deliberate intention of securing an advantage over us.

In foreign affairs, we have moved with timidity and indecision; we have tolerated Castro's name-calling and his confiscation of American property. The blood of American soldiers bought freedom for Cuba in the first place. American economic strength has supported Cuba. And I suggest it is always the nature of man who receives unearned benefits and undeserved charity to one day turn against his benefactor with a demand for more.

I am suggesting the Republican Party must determinedly maintain the most powerful military power in the world and that we must be willing to use this military power—and our economic power—to defend the rights of American citizens and to preserve American property.

I am reminding the Republican Platform Committee that private property and individual liberty are inseparable.

I am suggesting to the Republican Platform Committee that history has recorded that when a people become more concerned with their material possessions—and their sweet little luxuries—and their uneasy peace—they have inevitably fallen prey to destructive forces.

I am suggesting to the Republican Party the first responsibility of the federal government is to defend freedom—with all the force and power and resources at our command. I am suggesting that Russia is determined to achieve victory—that we have not been equally determined—and if Russia's ambition for world conquest will not be satisfied short of an aggressive war, then no amount of appeasement, no action short of surrender will satisfy the Russian ambition. And I am suggesting to the American people that if we truly desire to preserve freedom, we must be prepared to fight for its preservation if that eventuality becomes our last resort.

On two occasions in this century the world has been engulfed by war. Historians insist that both World War I and World War II were produced by miscalculation. They tell us that in both instances there probably would have been no general war had England, France and America made their position clearly known to the world.

Had these three great powers said: "We desire to keep the peace; we condemn war as a method of settling international disputes, we will attempt to understand the national aspirations of other countries. But if any nation or group of nations commits or permits to be committed certain acts, we will be forced to respond."

In our very recent experience it seems obvious there would have been no Korean War had the United States and the other members of the United Nations announced to the world in advance their intention of defending the integrity of South Korea.

What I am suggesting is, in my opinion, the most certain method by which war can be avoided. If we now declare to the rest of the world that our national conscience will not permit any invasion of the Western Hemisphere by either political or military means; if we announce to the world we will not countenance any aggression by either political or military means against any free nation; and if we back up this announcement with the superior military capacity we have and are capable of maintaining, then I suggest our enemy—Russian Communism—will not be encouraged to make any miscalculations which might involve the world in total destruction.

In domestic matters, I am reminding the members of the Republican Platform Committee that there is nothing new about a welfare state. History is littered with the remains of once-proud Republics who destroyed themselves by over-indulgence, by national acceptance of the false and destructive idea that you can get something for nothing.

The people of this Republic have not demanded federal assistance and federal handouts. The programs we have and the programs now being proposed are not the outgrowth of any public clamor or any demonstrable, widespread public need.

There has been no universal demand for federal aid-to-education. In fact, aside from the eloquent advocates of a small minority of school administrators, most people are opposed to federal aid to education.

There has been no widespread public demand for federal aid to depressed areas, or federal medical care for the aged, or federal support for the economy.

These programs have been seized on by ambitious politicians—after they were first advanced by various minority elements who appear determined to separate and divide the American people—to set the young against the aged, to pit the farmer against the consumer, to array the union member against the non-union member—to make success in any area the object of envy rather than admiration.

I am also reminding the Republican platform framers that in the discharge of my responsibility as Chairman of the Senatorial Campaign Committee, I have visited with Republican leaders and Republican voters in almost every state of the Union since the first of January, 1959.

In this connection, I have been constantly impressed by the concern of Republicans everywhere lest the Republican Party lose its identity in a mistaken effort to adopt the tactics and practices of the spend-and-spend, elect-and-elect architects of the New Deal and the Fair Deal.

In my opinion, the preservation of two strong political parties is essential to the preservation of the Republic. I am persuaded that the leaders of both parties long to keep America strong, to keep America free, to overcome misery and poverty and disease—to the end that all of our citizens may, in the future, enjoy a better life.

The difference between us is, I suggest, a difference in the methods we would follow to achieve these ojectives. Those currently in control of the Democrat Party appear to have given their allegiance to the concept of the superstate, with its perniciously paternalistic federal interference; with its dictatorial federal planning; committed to penalizing producers by the imposition of high taxes and distributing the benefits of the production of the energetic workers to those whose lack of initiative makes them eager recipients of governmental help.

I am suggesting it is the duty of government to help men who will help themselves—that to help and support men who will not help themselves is destructive.

I am urging the Republican Party to stand on those concepts of the functions and responsibility and *limitations* of the federal government which were established on this continent with the creation of the Republic of the United States. And I would suggest that we must work our way to a better tomorrow and to a peaceful world and that our objective can never be purchased through the sacrifice of individual freedom, accompanied by deficit financing and the stifling programs of a dictated society and a dictated economy.

## Suggested Declaration of Republican Principles

We, the people of the Republican Party, pledge our allegiance to that concept of the functions, responsibility and limitations of the federal government, established on this continent with the creation of the Republic of the United States.

We believe that in Communism and the centralization of government there is a very real and present danger which threatens to destroy freedom and to deny to all men their God-given individual dignity and rights.

We hold that all men are endowed by our Creator with freedom—to be responsible—to work in peace with justice toward all for a better tomorrow.

We hold it is the first responsibility of the federal government to protect the freedoms of citizens equally against attack and tyranny from without or within.

We declare it is our intention to keep the defensive and offensive military forces of this nation superior to the attacking power of any potential aggressor or aggressors, regardless of the cost in dollars and manpower, to the end that liberty and freedom may be maintained.

In this regard, we recognize that the dictators of atheistic

Communism are vigorously prosecuting a war against the people of the free world by economic, military and political and psychological means. We intend to respond to these assaults with all the resources at our command and we propose to defeat these forces arrayed against us. We reject the notion that a stalemate satisfies our commitment to the cause of freedom. *We must proclaim for victory in the cold war.*

We denounce and condemn those who would, by practicing appeasement, lead us to piecemeal surrender of the rights and the dignity of free men. *Victory must be our goal.*

We regard the people of this Republic as competent, responsible individuals—fully capable of courageously facing the truth and willingly accepting their share of the task of preserving human freedom and human dignity.

We hold that freedom will be most surely safeguarded if the responsibility for making decisions is held close to the people. We deplore the trend to thrust all responsibility on a federal bureaucracy in Washington—and thus create a superstate.

We hold that freedom cannot long be maintained unless there is also maintained fiscal responsibility in the affairs of all governmental subdivisions. Excessive public spending is the historical prelude to the disintegration of national existence.

We condemn deficit financing and declare it is the responsibility of all public officials to practice economy and, except in cases of dire national emergency, to provide the people with a balanced budget.

We declare our belief that the custodians of government should make provision for the retirement of our present staggering national debt by establishing a budgeted item for this purpose and that to put off settling the obligations we have incurred is cowardly and destructive to our freedom.

We condemn the thirty years of federal tinkering and interference in the lives of the American farmers which has denied to these citizens an opportunity to earn a fair return for their productive efforts.

We believe government interference in the farm field is destroying that segment of American agriculture which these programs propose to help. We offer in support of this statement the fact that agricultural producers whose operations and products are not included in the present farm program are demonstrably better off than are those unfortunate segments of the agricultural producers whose activities are now dictated and subsidized by the federal government.

We proclaim it is the responsibility of the federal government to restore economic freedom to all farmers. If this transition from a controlled agricultural economy to a free agricultural economy should create temporary hardship, we believe it is the responsibility of the federal government to offer temporary assistance, but this assistance must be limited and must be terminated within the specified period of years allocated to the transitional period.

We affirm our belief in the rights of any group to join together in voluntary association for improvement of wages or working conditions.

We condemn the concentration of power in the hands of a few unconscionable men who have invaded the American labor movement. And we pledge the support of the federal government to the restoration of democratic processes in those unions where dictatorial practices now exist.

We condemn those self-seekers who have sought to distort the legitimate labor union movement in this country and create an instrument of political and economic power—to be directed against the consumers, producers and the public. And we propose to correct the sources of these powers which exist in federal laws.

We condemn the concentration of power in the hands of business where it is used in a manner inimical to the best interests of the public. We deplore the concentration of power in the hands of federal bureaus—whose officials frequently operate without let or hindrance and with little regard for the opinions expressed by the people in democratic elections.

We declare our faith in the free enterprise competitive system as the best possible instrument for providing and distributing material needs and material benefits to all citizens.

We believe that any government or political system which seeks to level all men to a common standard of achievement by penalizing ability, initiative and thrift, is guilty of opposing God's will and our expressed recognition of the source of our freedoms.

We believe any society which proposes to relieve its citizens of all responsibility—and thus condemn them to a state of perpetual childhood—is acting contrary to the best purposes for mankind.

We believe every man is entitled to an equal position on the starting line in the race for personal achievement. But no man is to be guaranteed a preferred position at the finish line.

We believe energy, ability and a willingness to work for personal achievement are entitled to recognition and reward.

We believe that to tell men cynically they can get something for nothing is wrong . . .

... that to buy votes by legislating benefits for some at the expense of others is wrong ...

... that to incite the envy of one group of citizens for another is wrong ...

... that downgrading those virtues of thrift, honesty, self-reliance and reverence for the wisdom of tradition is to court disaster.

Our aim is to achieve justice for all men, to require responsible citizen participation in the affairs of government; to support voluntarism rather than compulsion; pluralism rather than centralization; and freedom rather than a controlled, falsely paternalistic government.

We hold that our nation can survive only by the united efforts of free men—supported by religious faith—practicing fidelity to our traditions—exhibiting integrity in public office—and displaying an unwavering love of country.

*Herewith is reprinted a guest article by Senator Goldwater from the August 1, 1960 issue of* Newsweek Magazine. *While this was written many weeks before the Presidential Election, it is easy to detect the Senator's concern lest uncompromising principles of Republican Party were not embraced.*

—THE EDITORS

The Republicans can win the election in 1960 by standing unequivocally and uncompromisingly on the traditional principles of the Republican Party.

I am convinced we will lose the 1960 elections if we embrace the false notion that a majority of American citizens are eager to trade their birthright of responsible freedom for the mess-of-pottage promise of subsidy and support.

The true Republican philosophy is a dynamic, compelling doctrine dealing with the full nature of man. It is the living, unquenchable spirit of the American Revolution. The touchstone is freedom.

In recent years it has become increasingly difficult for the average voter to find any basic difference between the parties. And I believe the resultant frustration has contributed to the creation of an apathetic attitude toward political decisions. A candidate's smile, personality or television image often tips the balance. This conclusion is supported by all national elections since 1940.

When the Republican Party has offered candidates and policies which were little more than hollow echoes of the siren songs of the welfare staters, the American voter—feeling defrauded of any opportunity to make a real choice—has displayed an indifference to the whole process of self-government.

The outcome of the 1952 election has been rationalized as being no more than the victory of Eisenhower, a popular war hero, over Stevenson, a relatively unknown governor. But I suggest it is folly to disregard the outcome in 1956.

The Democrat candidate, Stevenson, was the darling of the liberals. The campaign in 1952 had made him well known to the American voter. The health of the Republican incumbent had become an issue. And yet the best Adlai Stevenson could do was to gather about 26 million votes—and this, I would remind you is a clear loss of 1 million votes over the Democrat total in 1940.

If the super-state welfare programs of the radical liberal truly express the aspirations of the independent voter, then where were these independent voters in 1956 when Stevenson's candidacy offered an opportunity for a liberal victory?

As the victims of a world-wide depression in 1932, the American people were eager for a change—willing to experiment and hopeful of finding a political answer to their economic distress.

Many of the reforms of the Roosevelt Administration were long overdue—liberalization of credit for the home buyer under FHA; closer governmental supervision and support of the nation's banking system; and a system of providing compensation to those who are willing to work over a period of unemployment. All of these are now an accepted part of public policy, deserving to be strengthened and not abandoned. They stand in danger of being destroyed by the reckless expansion of governmental interference in the Democrat platform of 1960, that document of destruction which the delegates of the Democrat Party were forced to adopt at their convention in Los Angeles—a something-for-nothing program for the socialistic destruction of the free-enterprise system.

I have profound respect for the wisdom and judgment of the American people. We are not ready to substitute socialism under any mask or disguise for the benefits of freedom.

To win the elections of 1960, the Republicans must once again proclaim their devotion to a limited government which is the servant and not the master of the people. We must encourage men to lofty aspirations, to reach upward to the stars for themselves. We must proclaim again the dignity of work, the strengthening benefits of struggle—for life was not meant to be easy.

In striking contrast, the narrow, limited, material goals of the superstate socialism advocated by Senator Kennedy will become tawdry and cheap.

The Republican Party believes in fiscal responsibility in

governmental affairs, not because we are devoted to a book-keeper's figures, but because we know that any government which lives beyond its income and indulges its selfish appetites is creating disaster for its people.

The Republican Party believes in the pluralism and limited central authority established by the founders of this constitutional republic because we know that excessive governmental power inevitably destroys and enslaves its subjects.

The Republican Party, recognizing the right of any individual to cherish his own beliefs and notions, welcomes divergence of opinion on many issues.

I think the general public has found it difficult to recognize the true image of the Republican Party because the press and the commentators constantly emphasize the differences in viewpoints held by leading Republicans. Thus Mr. Rockefeller is customarily pictured as far to the Left while I am characterized as far to the Right.

The truth is that while Governor Rockefeller and I do disagree on many points, our areas of agreement far outweigh our areas of disagreement. And I would suggest that despite Governor Rockefeller's recent apparent criticism of Mr. Nixon, these two men are committed to the same objective and their areas of agreement are far more significant than the differences between them.

The Republicans will win the elections of 1960 by speaking honestly and sincerely to the American people; by offering a clear-cut choice; by resisting every temptation to compromise on welfare-state proposals; by refusing to engage in petty disputes over minor differences; by offering voters of America an opportunity to guarantee the continuation of the magnificent freedom, the unequalled opportunity of living as responsible citizens of the republic.

*A few places Barry Goldwater has been invited to speak:*
Point Clear, Mobile, Alabama Young Presidents Organization
Franklin Street Methodist Church, Johnstown, Pennsylvania
Woodstock College, Woodstock, Maryland
Holy Cross, Worcester, Mass.
Kenyon College, Gambier, Ohio
Dutch Treat Club, New York, N.Y.
Salvation Army Dinner, Statler Hotel, Los Angeles, Calif.
Mass. Institute of Technology Faculty Club, Boston, Mass.
City of Lake Forest Centennial Dinner, Lake Forest, Ill.
Catholic University Club, Chicago, Ill.
Lawrenceville School, Lawrenceville, New Jersey
Junior Chamber of Commerce, Young Man of Year Banquet,
 Williamsport, Pa.
Young Americans for Freedom, New York, N.Y.
Saints and Sinners, Korean Hotel, Miami, Florida
Rochester, N.Y., New York City Club
Wabash College, Crawfordsville, Ind.
St. Francis College, Brooklyn, N.Y.
Iowa State Automobile Dealers, Des Moines, Iowa
Georgetown College, Danford Thomas Lecture, George-
 town, Ky.
D.A.R., Constitution Hall, Washington, D.C.
Grinnell College, Grinnell, Iowa
Harvard Law School Forum, Cambridge, Mass.
Boston College Law Forum, Brighton, Mass.
Arizona State Commencement Address, Tempe, Arizona
Commencement Address, Brigham University, Provo, Utah
Commencement Address, Ashville School, Ashville, N.C.
Annual Convention, National Assn. Plumbing Contractors,
 Detroit, Mich.

Virginia State Bar Assn., Greenbrier, White Sulphur Springs, Va.

United Press International Conference of Editors & Publishers, Washington, D.C.

Vassar College, Poughkeepsie, N.Y.

Harvard Business Men's Club, New York, N.Y.

Richmond, Va., Junior Chamber of Commerce